Endorsements

This book should be called "Flatbread Fabulous" – but it's clearly bigger than that. From scratch or not, crisp or soft, thin or thick, sweet or savory, there's a "dough" for all occasions, whether serving appetizers to house-guests or meals to family. Choose Shelley's error-proof dough (plain, gluten-free or spiked with herbs, cheese or nuts), or grab a grocery store short-cut, and your breadbasket will be forever transformed. Shelley's internationally inspired recipes turn an ordinary staple into extraordinary gourmet food.

—Robin Miller,
TV Personality, Cookbook Author, Nutritionist

Internationally inspired Flatbreads made simple. This amazing cookbook offers delicious and healthy ways to enjoy foods from around the world, without ever leaving your kitchen. I'm always looking for creative ideas to make meals without all the fuss and calories, and *Skinny Bread* does just that.

—Akira Beck,
Executive Chef and Partner, Yellow Tail, Bellagio Hotel Las Vegas

Shelley is a one of those rare breeds that can do it all from writing cook books, being a TV personality, planning a Culinary Festival, teaching others to coo, etc. You get the idea. I am amazed Food Network hasn't offered her a show yet. Shelley makes learning these recipes easy and fun, and seeing her create these recipes live is truly a great experience everyone should enjoy. This is a great book and I love the easy and fun recipes. Who knew cooking flatbreads could be so fun!

—Joe Zanovitch,
Festival Director, Scottsdale Culinary Festival

The Skinny Bread

100 Ways to Make Flatbreads Plus Delicious and Healthy Pizzas, Tacos, Wraps, Focaccia, Crepes and More

Shelley Sikora-Holman

Published by Tate Publishing & Enterprises, LLC
127 E. Trade Center Terrace | Mustang, Oklahoma 73064 USA
1.888.361.9473 | www.tatepublishing.com

Tate Publishing is committed to excellence in the publishing industry. The company reflects the philosophy established by the founders, based on Psalm 68:11,
"The Lord gave the word and great was the company of those who published it."

Book design copyright © 2013 by Tate Publishing, LLC. All rights reserved.
Cover design by Matias Alasagas
Interior design by Joana Quilantang

Published in the United States of America

ISBN: 978-1-62147-496-8
13.03.19

TABLE OF CONTENTS

Dedication

This book is dedicated to St. Lorenzo, the patron saint of cooks and patron of the Florence Cooking School in Italy. He was a seventeenth-century Christian saint known for his classic grill and garlic, and who in the face of being condemned to death by fire called out to persecutors, "Turn me over. I'm done on this side."

Acknowledgments

This beautiful cookbook is truly a labor of love, and I am very excited to share these recipes with you! I have spent over two years researching flatbreads as a delicious, fast, and healthy alternative to traditional bread. A special thanks to all of my "golfing buddies" that participated in helping test these recipes (and their husbands, too)!

Thank you to the incredible staff at Tate Publishing for their support and creative suggestions.

And special thanks to Margo Kesler and Grant Crone, my media and publicists friends at MMPR Marketing, Phoenix, AZ. Without their steadfast belief in this project, I would not have persevered.

And last but not least, to the person who is the most important, supportive, and loved man in my life, Bob Holman. I thank all of you.

Introduction

Flatbread is both ancient and modern.

This cookbook is your complete recipe source for quick and easy flatbreads plus grilled pizzas, wraps and sandwiches, crackers and crostini, focaccia and calzones—and don't forget delicious flatbread desserts.

These recipes are for simple bread dough made of flour, water, and salt then rolled or flattened, unleavened, or made with yeast. The bread can be thin and crisp or spongy in texture, and baked or grilled.

Historians track its origins to 10,000 years ago when wheat was harvested, ground, doused with a little water, stirred into dough, and baked on rocks. Today, flatbreads can be baked in less than thirty minutes, or quicker yet bought at most any grocery store, and with a few ingredients and ingenuity, it can be turned into a meal.

Either way, today's "fast breads" offer a no-fuss way to get dinner on the table and to serve as appetizers to friends or feed the soccer team lunch. The bread that began as a survival food remains so today. It's the go-to bread for those with little time to cook. These thin, dense breads offer a refreshing and lower carbohydrate alternative to loaves typically served in the mealtime breadbasket. When topped with radicchio and whipped ricotta or lobster and goat cheese, flatbreads quickly transform from side to main dish. For cooks with no time or desire to master the time-consuming art of baking bread, these thin, dense breads fit the bill. No "knead" to stress. Flatbreads also offer a lower carbohydrate and lower calorie option for those unwilling to forgo breads. Flatbread is simple to make and quicker than quick-bread but way more interesting. It can be thought of somewhere between a cracker and pizza, crisp and thin or soft and chewy.

The *Skinny Bread Cookbook* teaches how to bake low-fat, healthy flatbreads with a few baking steps and ingredients, with no leavening and no waiting. This book also shows how to turn these flatbreads into appetizers, meals, snacks, and desserts using either flatbreads baked from scratch or bought from the grocery store's well-stocked shelves.

The *Skinny Bread Cookbook* celebrates flatbreads as side dishes and elevates them to main dishes, whether grilled or baked in the oven and served either savory or sweet.

A Passion for Flatbread

I became obsessed with flatbreads before the now-popular bread alternative began gracing tables at mainstream restaurants.

True confessions: I'm a carb-aholic who was looking for an alternative to satisfy my craving for traditional loaf bread. My fix became the lower-carb alternative of flatbreads. In no time, I traded traditional loafs for flatbreads. Before I knew it, my passion for flatbread morphed into a healthy eating lifestyle, with friends and family quickly jumping on board.

The Skinny on Flatbread

In Mexico it is called a tortilla; in France, crepe and fougasse; in Italy, Piadina and focaccia; in India, naan; and in Greece, pita. The familiarity of flatbread covers centuries and continents. Its versatility is hard to match. Flatbread handles a sandwich perfectly. It also doubles as pizza crust or cracker for dips and spreads. Its range runs from appetizer to main entrée to dessert.

This is a cookbook that offers easy recipes, offering alternative ways to make flatbreads. Flatbreads are portable, flexible, healthy, and easily made gluten-free. You don't have to be a bread baker to enjoy the satisfying taste of homemade or store-bought flatbreads. No bread machine needed here. These recipes will take you on a delicious, sweet, and savory adventure the entire family will enjoy.

The *Skinny Bread Cookbook* is easy to read, and the recipes and ingredients are readily available in supermarkets.

Tips and Guidelines

Tools and Tips of the Trade

Tips

Outdoor Grilling – Nothing provides deep, smoky flavors better than cooking flatbreads on an outdoor grill. Whether using gas or charcoal, you'll be pleased by the hard-to-beat flavor. For the best flavors and crispiest bread, use charcoal briquettes or natural wood.

Indoor Grilling – I have long been a fan of indoor grilling, especially as an alternative to outside grilling during the long hot nights of summertime in the desert. I can attest that owning a great cast-iron grill pan also produces flatbread as good as its outdoor counterpart.

Temperature – Whether baking indoors or out, temperature matters. The recommended temp for the perfect crust is 500 degrees.

Thin Crust – Use less dough and stretch the crust to the desired size for a thinner crust. Or for a drier, denser, and crispier crust, reduce the amount of water.

Thicker Crust – Try using a pizza pan if oven baking, or a stove-top pan, so that you can control the size and thickness you want. You can also achieve this result when using an outdoor grill. If you like a soft and chewy crust, use less flour. A moist crust produces a softer crust. Flour with a low gluten content or even gluten-free flour will also produce this same result.

Altitude – Baking in the mountains or at the beach affects the dough. The higher the altitude, the less air pressure, makes dough rise faster. Adding a bit more water helps slow down the cooking time.

Tools

Pizza Stone – Whether for baking or grilling, a pizza stone provides the evenly heated surface necessary to absorb moisture from the flatbread/pizza and turns out a thin, crispy crust. The thickness of the stone promotes the consistent baking required for yeast crusts and encourages the dough to rise slowly and evenly.

Pizza Screen – This gadget will help you create the perfect pizza. Screens are usually circular in shape and made of aluminum or stainless steel and have perforated holes that allow the hot air to circulate, allowing the dough to cook more evenly.

Wood Pizza Peel – This is a great tool for either baking inside or grilling outdoors. The surface of a peel is wide enough to allow for easy sliding and removing dough. The long handle length is also great because it prevents you from reaching over open flames or into a hot oven for the dough.

Pizza Cutter Wheel – This is a must for cutting uniform slices of pieces without having to touch the hot dough. For an alternative, I use kitchen scissors, which performs just as well.

Tongs – Tongs are very useful when grilling outdoors. I prefer 14" to 16" tongs that help shield my hands from the open flames.

Baking Terms

Bake– To cook in an oven with dry heat. Always heat the oven for 10-15 minutes before baking.

Combine – To stir together two or more ingredients until mixed.

Cut in – To distribute solid fat throughout the dry ingredients using a pastry blender, fork, or a food processor.

Dash – A measurement less than 1/8 teaspoon.

Dough – A soft, thick mixture of flour and liquid.

Drizzle – To drip a glaze over food from the tines of a fork or the end of a spoon.

Dust – To sprinkle lightly with sugar, flour, or cocoa.

Fold in – To gently combine heavy and delicate mixtures, such as a beaten egg white or whipped cream, without causing loss of air.

Knead – To fold, push, or turn dough to produce a smooth, elastic texture.

Lukewarm – A temperature of about 105 degrees. It should feel neither hot nor cold.

Mix – To stir together two or more ingredients until thoroughly combined.

SHELLEY SIKORA-HOLMAN

Mix until moistened – To combine dry ingredients with liquid ingredients until the dry ingredients are thoroughly moistened, with the mixture remaining slightly lumpy.

Proof – To allow yeast dough to rise before baking. Or, to dissolve yeast in warm liquid and set it in a warm place for 5 to 10 minutes to allow it to expand and bubble.

Refrigerate – To chill in the refrigerator until a mixture is cool, or a dough is firm.

Stir – To combine ingredients in a circular motion with a spoon or whisk.

Toss – To mix lightly with a lifting motion, using two forks or spoons.

The Dough

For the best flavor, making flatbread dough from scratch is the way to go. Thankfully, most recipes are simple, requiring time to rise and a couple of kneads. But for those short on time, frozen pizza is a suitable alternative. The good news: You decide which works for you.

Chef's Tip: When preparing prepared or from-scratch dough, roll out gently. The more the dough is handled, the tougher it turns out. Gentle kneading leaves the necessary air bubbles in place to produce tender dough and luscious bread.

PART ONE

Savory Flatbreads

Flatbread has a long, storied history for a reason. Whether whole wheat sourdough, flavored with chive and parsley, cheddar cheese or gluten-free, flatbreads are easy to make. An added bonus: they are healthy and feed our souls. Make them flat, or for a stunning presentation, in a bowl.

Basic Flatbread Dough

You do not have to have a baking stone for crusty bread. But what the stone does is help distribute the heat a little more evenly. Adding moisture or steam is what makes a crunchy crust. One trick is to try adding a little water to a baking pan or dish and place it on the bottom shelf of your oven or use a mister and spray water in the oven during the first few minutes of baking. Try it.

Makes 2, 12-inch crust

Ingredients
 2/3 cup warm water (105 to 115 degrees)
 1 packet active dry yeast
 2 tablespoons sugar
 1/4 cup extra-virgin olive oil
 2 cups all purpose (unbleached) flour, plus more for dusting
 1/2 teaspoon salt

Directions
 In a small bowl, combine the warm water and sprinkle with the yeast. Let stand until foamy, about 5 minutes. Whisk sugar, salt, and half the olive oil into yeast mixture. Add flour and stir until a sticky dough forms. Pour the remaining olive oil into the bottom of the bowl, and turn the dough over so the oil is on both the top and bottom. Use hands to shape into a ball. Cover bowl with plastic wrap and a clean dish towel to prevent air from getting into the bowl, and set aside in a draft-free place until the dough has doubled in size, about 1 hour. Punch dough down and turn onto a lightly floured surface. Divide in half. Cover and let rest for ten minutes, then place one of the pieces of dough on a floured work surface and either use a rolling pin to stretch the dough to a 12-inch circle, or stretch by hand creating an artisan-style free-form circle, and repeat with the second piece.

SHELLEY SIKORA-HOLMAN

Basic Flatbread Grilling Instructions

For outdoor grilling, heat up grill to approximately 400 degrees. When hot, lightly oil grill. Place evwwach dough round on a mesh round pizza screen, and stretch to desired size. Transfer directly onto hot grill.

Grill about 3 minutes, looking for bubbles. Being careful not to tear the crust, lift one side to make sure there are golden brown grill marks. If ready, pick up the crust from the center with tongs, and place back on the pizza screen grilled side face-up. Place toppings on grilled side, then place back on the grill to finish cooking, about 3-5 minutes.

Can't grill outdoors? No problem. Place the dough on a cast-iron grill pan for stove-top cooking or place onto a pizza stone for oven baking at about 500 degrees until golden brown.

No-Yeast Whole Wheat Sourdough

I've made this several times and it always turns out good. Just make sure you knead the dough for the required amount of time.

Makes 6 individual flatbreads

Ingredients

1 cup unbleached all-purpose flour

2 teaspoons salt

1/4 cup vegetable oil

1/2 cup assorted seeds such as sesame, caraway, fennel, poppy seeds

2 cups whole wheat or white wheat flour

4 teaspoons sourdough bread enhancer

1 1/4 cup, or about 10-12 ounces water

1 tablespoon salt

Directions

Bread machine method: Place flours, salt, sourdough bread enhancer, oil, and water in the bread machine. Program for white bread and press "start." Knead until a soft, pliable ball of dough forms, adjusting flour or liquid if necessary. Cancel the machine at the end of the first knead cycle.

Food processor method: Place the flours, salt, and sourdough bread enhancer in the work bowl of the food processor fitted with the plastic blade. With the machine on, gradually add the oil and then the water. When a ball of dough forms, process for 40 seconds. The dough should be soft and pliable. Remove and allow dough to rest 15 minutes.

Preheat oven to 475 degrees and place rack in the upper third of the oven. Lightly coat a heavy baking sheet with nonstick vegetable spray. Divide the dough into 6 pieces. While working with each piece, keep remaining dough covered with a clean dish towel. Sprinkle the work surface with a generous amount of seeds and pat into the dough. Roll the dough in a free-form shape, as thin as possible, then transfer to prepared pan and continue rolling until paper thin. Bake for 5-7 minutes or until the edges are crisp and brown, and the center has risen unevenly and bubbled. Cool on racks and store uncovered at room temperature.

SHELLEY SIKORA-HOLMAN

Gluten-Free Dough

Gluten is a protein found in wheat flour. It is what makes traditional bread dough chewy and allows it to rise. For those who cannot tolerate gluten, a substitute is needed. Try this recipe for a fuss-free bread, pizza, or flatbread.

Makes 6 servings

Ingredients
  1 cup brown rice flour
  1/2 cup corn starch (or potato flour if available)
  1/4 cup arrowroot
  2 teaspoons granulated sugar
  1 teaspoon xanthan gum
  1/4 cup extra-virgin olive oil, divided in half
  1 cup buttermilk
  Cornmeal or polenta for dusting
  1 teaspoon sea salt

Directions
    In the bowl of a stand mixer, using a dough hook, combine flour, corn starch, arrowroot, sugar, xanthan gum, half extra-virgin olive oil, and salt. Gradually add the milk until the dough forms a soft and smooth ball. Don't use all the buttermilk unless needed to soften dough, but dough should not be too sticky.
    Sprinkle cornmeal on a work surface. Divide the dough into six equal pieces and roll each into a ball. Using a rolling pin, roll out each to form a 10-inch circle. Heat heavy skillet or grill pan on medium heat and add the remaining oil. Cook each dough separately, until golden brown, or about 1-2 minutes per side. Drain on paper towel. Set aside and keep warm. This dough can be used to replace any of the dough recipes in this cookbook.

Hazelnut Dough

A hazelnut is the nut of the hazel and is also known as a cob nut or filbert nut. I don't know about you, but I love the flavor, and hazelnuts rich in protein and unsaturated fat.

Makes 2, 12-inch crusts

Ingredients
   1 cup warm water, about 105 -115 degrees
   1 package active dry yeast
   1 tablespoon sugar
   1/4 cup extra-virgin olive oil, divided in half
   2 cups unbleached all-purpose flour, plus extra for dusting
   1/2 cup hazelnut meal (see recipe below)
   1 tablespoon freshly chopped thyme or rosemary, optional

Directions
   In a small bowl, place warm water and sprinkle in yeast. Combine until frothy. Whisk in sugar and half of the olive oil. Add flour and hazelnut meal, and optional thyme or rosemary. Mix together until the dough forms into a ball. Pour the remaining oil into the bottom of the bowl, and knead until combined. Cover bowl with plastic wrap and a clean dish towel. Set aside in a draft-free, warm location for about 1 hour or until doubled in size.
   Divide the dough into two equal halves, cover, and set aside until ready to stretch. Top and follow basic directions to bake or grill.
   For hazelnut meal, grind about 1/4 pound skinned and toasted hazelnuts in a nut mill until the meal has the consistency of cornmeal. Or use a food processor fitted with a steel blade, being careful to prevent the meal from turning into nut butter. Tips: Freeze the nuts before grinding, use the pulse setting on the processor, and add a little sugar to the nuts to help absorb the oils. Store nut meal in the refrigerator or freezer, and use soon after purchase and grinding. One-quarter pound of ground whole nuts yields about 1 cup nut meal. Reserve remaining for later use.

SHELLEY SIKORA-HOLMAN

Fresh Herb Dough

It's so easy to make your own pizza dough. Once you do, you can begin to experiment with a variety of fresh herbs out of your garden that add flavor to plain crusts.

Makes 16 individual flatbreads

Ingredients
    1 cup warm water (105-115 degrees)
    1 package active dry yeast
    2 tablespoons sugar
    3 cups unbleached all-purpose flour, plus extra for dusting
    2 teaspoons coarse salt or flavored salt (fleur de sel), plus extra for topping
    1/4 cup extra-virgin olive oil
    1 large egg whisked with 1 teaspoon water for egg wash
    1/2 cup fresh, whole herbs (basil, parsley, rosemary, or a mixture of the herbs of your choice)

Directions
    In a small bowl combine warm water and sprinkle with yeast. Stir until frothy and bubbles form, about 5 minutes. Add sugar, flour, and salt, and stir together until dough forms. Place oil in bottom of bowl and add dough. Knead with the oil until combined. Cover with plastic wrap and a clean dish towel, and place in a draft-free warm location for about 1 hour, or until doubled in size.
    Preheat the oven to 350 degrees. Divide dough into 16 equal pieces, and place on a cookie sheet. Cover with plastic wrap and let rest for about 10 minutes. Lightly flour a clean work surface and roll out each piece, one at a time, or hand stretch to about a 10-inch rectangle. Transfer each flatbread dough sheet to a parchment-lined cookie sheet, about four per cookie sheet. Brush each with egg wash, flavored salt and fresh herbs. Bake until crisp and golden brown for about 15-18 minutes. Let cool and transfer to a container for up to 3 days.
    Serve with a hot soup or a cold salad.

Herb Flatbread

Honey Black Pepper Dough

A little sweet goes perfectly with a little spice. In this case a little fresh ground black pepper, will add just enough flavor without a lot of heat.

Makes 16 individual flatbreads

Ingredients
    3 cups unbleached all-purpose flour
    2 teaspoons baking powder
    1 teaspoon sea salt
    1 cup hot water from tap
    3 tablespoons honey, plus 2 tablespoons
    1/4 cup cold water (reserve)
    1/2 cup vegetable oil for frying
    1 teaspoon coarsely ground black pepper

Directions
    In a food processor, mix together flour, baking powder, and salt. Reserve. In a small bowl, combine hot water and 3 tablespoons of honey. With machine running, pour water mixture into bowl; process until dough forms a ball. Use reserve cold water if needed to form an elastic-type dough. Turn out dough onto a lightly floured work surface. Knead for 2 to 3 minutes or until dough comes together and is soft but not sticky. Add a little more flour if necessary.
    Divide the dough into 16 equal pieces and shape into balls. Roll out each one into a 6-inch circle. Add oil to a large fry pan or skillet, and heat over medium heat. Place dough into pan, one at a time, and cook until slightly browned or about 1 minute on each side.
    Warm remaining 2 tablespoons of honey in the microwave for about 15 seconds. Brush warmed honey on one side of each bread, and lightly sprinkle with pepper and salt to taste. Repeat with remaining breads. Cool completely and serve as a side accompaniment in place of regular bread or as a cracker with dips and spreads.

Cheddar Cheese Dough

Who doesn't love cheddar cheese? If your family is like mine, they will have no problem diving into a delicious, homemade flatbread crust that isn't too gooey, but bursts with the flavor and aroma of cheddar cheese.

Makes 12 individual flatbreads.

Ingredients

- 1 package active dry yeast
- 3/4 cup warm milk (same temperature as water)
- 1/4 cup unsalted butter, melted
- 1 1/2 teaspoon salt
- 1/4 cup extra-virgin olive oil
- 1/2 teaspoon paprika
- 1/4 teaspoon celery seed
- 1 cup sharp cheddar cheese, shredded
- 1/4 cup warm water (105-115 degrees)
- 2 tablespoons unsalted butter room temperature
- 1 tablespoon sugar
- 2 1/2-3 cups unbleached all-purpose flour
- 2 tablespoons minced dried onion
- 1/2 teaspoon dried oregano
- 1/4 teaspoon garlic salt

Directions

In a small mixing bowl, dissolve yeast in warm water. Add milk, butter, sugar, and salt. Stir in enough flour to form a ball. Lightly flour a clean work surface, and knead dough until smooth and elastic. Place olive oil in the bowl. Add dough and knead into the oil and form a ball. Cover with plastic wrap and a clean dish towel, and place in a draft-free warm location until dough is doubled in size, or about 1 hour. Punch dough down and divide in half. Press each half in a greased 9-inch pie plate.

Preheat oven to 350 degrees.

In a small bowl, combine melted butter and seasonings, and then brush over the dough. Place dough on large baking sheets.

Sprinkle with the cheddar cheese. Using a fork, prick the dough several times to prevent bubbles from forming. Cover and let rise another 30 minutes. Bake for 20-25 minutes or until golden brown. When cool remove from pans and place on wire rack. Serve as a side accompaniment to soup or salads, or serve as an appetizer. Flatbread may be stored in a covered container and refrigerated for up to 3 days.

SHELLEY SIKORA-HOLMAN

Chive-Parsley Dough

Perfect blends of flavors, chives are a mild flavored herb and can be found fresh at most markets year-round, making them a readily available herb; they can also be dry-frozen without much impairment to the taste.

Makes 12 individual flatbreads

Ingredients
   1/2 cup warm water (105-115 degrees)
   2 teaspoons active dry yeast
   2 teaspoons sugar, divided
   2 teaspoon sea salt, divided
   2 cups unbleached all-purpose flour
   1/4 cup extra-virgin olive oil, divided (set aside 2 tablespoons for brushing top of dough)
   4 tablespoon unsalted butter, cubed and cold
   1 large egg, plus 1 egg yolk

Directions
   Combine 2 cups finely chopped chives, 1/2 cup finely chopped fresh flat leaf parsley (or you can use cilantro), and 1/2 cup sesame seeds, set aside.
   In a small bowl, combine warm water and sprinkle with yeast. Stir until frothy and bubbles form, about 5 minutes, then combine with flour, butter, and salt and sugar in the bowl of a stand mixer. Using a dough hook, add butter and beat in egg, yolk, and yeast mixture until combined. Knead at medium speed until dough forms a soft and elastic dough ball. In a large bowl, add the olive oil and knead until combined into the dough. Cover and place in a draft-free area until dough doubles in size.
   Preheat oven to 350 degrees.
   Using a rolling pin, roll out the dough on a lightly floured work surface to a rectangle shape about the size of 18x10-inch. Spoon herb mixture evenly onto center and spread mixture to corners of dough. Working from one short edge, roll dough into a long tube shape. Cut into 2-inch slices. Transfer slices, cut end up, onto a greased cookie sheet. Brush tops with remaining oil and seed toppings. Bake until golden brown for about 30 minutes. Serve warm.

The Flatbread Bowl

Bread-bowls aren't just for restaurants. This is my favorite way of impressing friends, is by making this fabulous, "edible" bread bowl, yet so easy if you are using store-bought pizza dough. Just shape it by turning over an oven-safe bowl and bake it!

Bread Bowl

SHELLEY SIKORA-HOLMAN

Flatbread Bowl

Makes 1 bowl

Ingredients
    1 store-bought refrigerated pizza dough (enough to make a 12-14" pizza) or substitute a flatbread recipe
    1 quart oven-proof bowl and 1 cookie sheet pan
    Nonstick oil spray
    1-2 tablespoons cornmeal
    1 tablespoon unsalted butter, or extra-virgin olive oil (optional)

Directions
    Preheat the oven to 450 degrees. Using store-bought pizza dough, roll out to about a 12-inch circle.
    Turn oven-proof, soup-size bowl upside down and place on a cooking sheet. Spray or brush the outside of the bowl with a nonstick cooking spray. Sprinkle the outer surface of the dough with the cornmeal. Drape the dough over the bowl, making sure the entire bowl is covered. Pinch the edges of the dough to form a rustic, ribbon-like pie edge. Be careful not to press the dough too hard, or else it may stick. Place the covered dough bowl and cookie sheet in oven, and bake for about 15 minutes or until lightly brown. Option: Brush the finished bowl inside and top edges with extra-virgin olive oil for flavor. Set aside until cool. Place in a sealed container for up to 1 week or until ready to serve.

Tortilla Bread Bowl

Bread-bowls made from tortillas are traditional used for taco salads, so why not try something different with one of your favorite salads by replacing your everyday ceramic bowl.

Makes 4-6 bowls

Ingredients:
  1 pan for 12 muffins
  4-6 flour or whole wheat tortillas (corn sticks to the pan)
  1 tablespoon extra-virgin olive oil

Directions
  Preheat oven to 375 degrees. Turn upside down a 12-muffin pan. Place a tortilla between two of the raised muffin cups by forming a round bowl. Seal the edges that touch together with a little olive oil. Bowls will not be perfectly round but will have a rustic look. Bake for about 6-8 minutes or until you have golden brown crispy shells.
  Gently remove and store in a sealed container for up to 1 week or until ready to serve.

Pita Bread Bowls

Pita bread isn't just for chips and sandwiches. Try making these small bread-bowl "cups" instead to serve your favorite fruit salad or dip.

Makes 4 bowls

Ingredients
    4 pita rounds
    8 cups canola oil

Directions
    Heat oil in a deep frying pot, to about 375 degrees.
    Leave pita breads in plastic wrap, and microwave for about 10 seconds until pliable. Place flatbread round in oil and hold it down under the surface with a long-handed metal ladle. When flatbread begins to curl up to form a bowl, about 2 minutes, and turns golden brown and crispy, remove with tongs. Drain on paper towels. Repeat frying with remaining flatbread.

PART TWO

Appetizers

These appetizers jump-start any meal with unorthodox flavors such as peanut butter hummus with honey baked pita chips or more traditional smoked salmon toasts. Either way, these flavor-packed bites fit the bill for appetizers at any gathering. Serve before a meal, or for a small plate's party, make and serve a variety, from roasted tomato cookies to chicken taquitos.

Sweet Vidalia Onion, Fennel, and Feta Tart

If you're asking yourself what is a "Vidalia onion, and is it really sweet?" The answer is yes. So when I was looking for different ways to use these sweeties, I came up with this tasty tart.

Makes 12 servings

Ingredients
    1 package of puff pastry, 2 sheets, thawed
    4 tablespoons unsalted butter
    5 pounds Vidalia onions, peeled and julienned
    1 1/2 pounds feta cheese, crumbled
    3/8 cup or about 3 ounces fresh tarragon, finely chopped
    3/8 cup or about 3 ounces fresh flat leaf parsley, finely chopped
    1/4 teaspoon fleur de sel salt
    1/4 teaspoon fresh ground black pepper
    1 small fennel bulb, peeled and shaved

Directions
    For the crust, preheat the oven to 400 degrees. To make onion and feta mixture, heat butter in a large skillet on medium heat. Cook until onions are tender. While onions are cooking, in a small bowl whisk feta and all remaining herbs, season with salt and pepper, and add to the onions and sauté for about 5 minutes.
    Roll out thawed puff pastry dough with a rolling pin on a lightly floured work surface. Place each rolled pastry sheet on a greased cookie sheet. Bake until almost done, about 15 minutes. Remove from oven and top with onion and feta, then spread fennel shavings over the top. Return to the oven and bake for about 10 more minutes or until bubbly.
    Serve warm.

SHELLEY SIKORA-HOLMAN

Peanut Butter Hummus
with Honey-Baked Pita Chips

Dip in! I love hummus, and I love peanut butter, so why not combine the two for a healthy duo-snack that is loaded with nutrients, and can also be used as an appetizer.

Makes 6 servings

Peanut Butter Hummus

Ingredients

1/4 cup extra-virgin olive oil

1 can, 16 ounces chickpeas, un-drained

3 tablespoons lemon juice

1 clove garlic

1 tablespoon finely chopped fresh flat leaf parsley

1/2 cup creamy peanut butter

1/4 cup finely chopped pine nuts

1 tablespoon sesame oil or 1/4 teaspoon crushed red pepper flakes

1/4 teaspoon sea salt

Directions

Place all ingredients, except the parsley, into a blender or food processor, and blend until smooth. Stir in parsley. Serve with baked pita chips; see recipe below.

Honey-Baked Pita Chips

Ingredients

2 tablespoons honey

6 small, 8-inch flour tortillas

2 teaspoons water

2 teaspoons sesame seeds

Directions

Preheat oven to 350 degrees. Cut each tortilla into 6 wedges. In a small bowl, stir together water and honey to loosen the honey. Place tortilla wedges on a baking sheet, brush with honey, and sprinkle with sesame seeds. Toast until golden brown and crisp, for about 15-18 minutes. Remove from oven and let cool.

Petite Passaladiere

Petite Passaladiere

Similar to an Italian pizza, with a slightly thicker crust, this delicious, rich and wonderful herbed onion, tomato, and olive tart originated in Provence, and lends itself to many variations of toppings.

Makes 18 appetizers

Ingredients
  1 tablespoon unsalted butter
  1 tablespoon extra-virgin olive oil
  2 large red onions, peeled and cut into small wedges
  1 teaspoon sugar
  1/4 teaspoon sea salt
  1/4 teaspoon fresh ground black pepper
  1/4 teaspoon crushed red pepper
  1/4 cup kalamata olives, pitted and chopped
  1 package puff pastry (2 sheets)
  1 dozen red and yellow heirloom grape or cherry tomatoes, halved
  1/4 cup feta cheese, crumbled
  Fresh tarragon sprigs for garnish

Directions
  Preheat oven to 400 degrees.
  Lightly grease 2 large cookie sheets. In a large skillet, heat butter and olive oil over medium heat. Add onions and cook until onions are tender. Stir in sugar, salt, and black and crushed red pepper. Cook for another 5 minutes or until onions appear golden brown. Stir in olives.
  On a lightly floured work surface, roll out the pasty sheets. Cut each sheet into 9 squares. Place each square on the prepared cookie sheet. Top with onion mixture and tomatoes. Bake for 20 minutes or until golden brown. Sprinkle with cheese, and garnish with tarragon sprigs.

Smoked Salmon Toasts

Nothing tastes better for a quick brunch snack or favorite appetizer, then fresh smoked salmon on a toasted slice of baguette bread.

Makes 10-12 servings

Ingredients
    1/2 cup cream cheese
    1 small shallot
    1 tablespoon chopped chives, plus one-inch lengths for garnish
    1 tablespoon chopped and drained capers
    1 tablespoon lemon juice
    1/4 teaspoon sea salt
    1/4 teaspoon fresh ground black pepper
    1 small baguette bread, diagonally sliced
    Extra-virgin olive oil for brushing
    1/2 pound smoked salmon, coarsely chopped
    Chive sprigs for garnish

Directions
    In a small bowl, combine cream cheese, shallots, chives, capers, and lemon juice. Add salt and pepper.
    Preheat oven to 400 degrees. Brush bread slices with extra-virgin olive oil. Toast in oven for about 5 minutes or until light golden brown.
    Top toasts with smoked salmon, and garnish with chive sprigs and serve.

SHELLEY SIKORA-HOLMAN

Crostini with Smoked Salmon

Sicilian Eggplant Flatbread with Roasted Peppers

Drawing from my Italian roots, you will be surprised how everyone will devour this easy yet elegant treat that's healthy and meatless.

Makes 6 servings

Ingredients

1/4 cup extra-virgin olive oil, divided in half
1 large eggplant, cut into 6 rounds, about 1/2-inch thick
1 loaf of Ciabatta bread, cut horizontally in half
1 1/4 cups chunky marinara sauce
1/2 cup chopped fresh basil, plus 6 leaves for garnish

2 ounces Chevre goat cheese
1 jar roasted red peppers
1 cup grated mozzarella cheese
Salt and pepper to taste

Directions

Preheat oven to 400 degrees. Heat half of the extra-virgin olive oil in a large skillet over medium heat. Sprinkle eggplant with salt and pepper. Place in skillet, cover, and cook until tender, about 10-15 minutes, turning as needed. Remove and transfer eggplant to a plate.

Brush cut sides of bread with the remaining olive oil. Place bread in another large skillet, with cut side down until brown and toasted.

Place bread, cut side up, on baking sheet. Spread with 3/4 cup sauce. Crumble and top with goat cheese, and sprinkle with chopped basil. Top with eggplant, peppers, and mozzarella cheese. Spoon remaining sauce over top.

Bake bread until topping is hot and crust is crisp for about 10 minutes. Cut into 6 pieces, and garnish with basil leaves.

Serve warm.

Parmesan Tuiles with Heirloom Tomato Bruschetta

A tuile is a thin, crisp, sweet or savory cookie or wafer made of dough or cheese. Originally from France, tuile or tiles, that line the rooftops of French country homes, particularly those in Provence, get their curved shape by placing them on a curved surface, such as a wine bottle or rolling pin.

Makes 12 servings

Ingredients
  1 1/2 cups grated parmesan cheese
  4 1/2 tablespoons unsalted butter, softened
  3 tablespoons, plus 6 teaspoons all-purpose flour, plus extra for pressing
  1/4 teaspoon fresh ground pepper
  5 cups finely diced heirloom cherry tomatoes, red and yellow
  1 tablespoon minced garlic
  3 teaspoons fresh basil, chopped
  1/4 cup extra-virgin olive oil

Directions
  Preheat oven to 400 degrees. Line a baking sheet with parchment paper. In a medium bowl, combine the cheese with butter, flour, and a black pepper. Mix together to form a dough. Then make into a log, cut into 36 equal slices, and arrange the slices on the baking sheet. Using your fingers, press the slices into 1-2 inch rounds. Flour your fingers to prevent sticking.
  Bake the tuiles on the bottom rack of oven for 6-7 minutes or until tuiles are sizzling and golden brown. Remove from oven and let cool completely, then transfer onto paper towels.
  In a bowl, toss the tomatoes with the garlic, basil, and olive oil, and then season to taste with salt and pepper. Spoon the bruschetta over top of the tuiles, and serve immediately.

Parmesan Cheese Tuiles

Savory Flatbread Cookies with Roasted Grape Tomatoes

Who said that cookies are only for dessert? In this case you will love the chance to try a savory flatbread version of this non-traditional appetizer.

Makes 12 Servings

Ingredients
  - 4 cups grape tomatoes
  - 3 cloves garlic, peeled
  - 3 tablespoons extra-virgin olive oil
  - 2 teaspoons coarse sea salt
  - 1 teaspoon fresh ground pepper
  - 2 1-pound store-bought refrigerated pizza dough's, or one of the dough recipes from this cookbook
  - 2 tablespoons fresh chopped basil
  - 1 teaspoon dried oregano
  - 14 ounces fresh mozzarella cheese, cut into 12 slices

Directions

For the roasted tomatoes, preheat oven to 400 degrees. In a medium bowl, add the tomatoes and garlic cloves. Drizzle with olive oil and sprinkle with salt and pepper. In a baking dish, place the tomatoes and garlic, and spread evenly to form one layer. Roast for 20 minutes and stir. Add 2-3 tablespoons of hot water if tomatoes appear dry. Return to oven and bake for an additional 20 minutes. When done, place in a small bowl and set aside.

(cont'd)

For the Flatbread

Roll out each pizza dough into a rectangle, or stretch by hand for a rustic artesian look. Cover with saran wrap and let rest for 10 minutes. Use a 2-inch round cookie cutter to cut out approximately 48 circles. Place the dough rounds on a lightly greased baking sheet.

In a small bowl, combine oil, oregano, and basil. Brush both sides of dough rounds with oil mixture, and prick with a fork to prevent bubbles.

Grill it. Light your grill and turn down to a medium fire. Use tongs to carefully place dough rounds on the grill, and grill for about 2 minutes on each side, lightly pressing down to flatten. Top each piece with a slice of cheese. Close grill and continue to cook until cheese melts, about 1 minute. Set aside on a covered plate to keep warm.

Bake it. Preheat oven to 450 degrees. Brush dough rounds with olive oil basil mixture, and bake on a greased baking sheet for 6-7 minutes. Flip and top with cheese. Return to oven and bake 2 minutes.

Top each round with a spoonful of roasted cherry tomatoes and basil, and serve warm.

SHELLEY SIKORA-HOLMAN

Mini BLT Pizzettas with Aged Goat Cheese

Why should pizza shops have all the fun? Here is a new twist on how to toss a perfect mini pie. It smells like pizza, it tastes like pizza, but it looks like it's been zapped by a shrinking machine! It's the pizzetta!

Makes 18 servings

Ingredients
   1 pound store-bought refrigerated pizza dough, or substitute a dough recipe
   Extra-virgin olive oil
   Sea salt and fresh ground pepper
   2 teaspoons fresh rosemary, coarsely chopped
   8 ounces Chevre goat cheese, cut into 35 thin wedges
   1/4 cup Kalamata olives, pitted and quartered
   18 cherry or grape tomatoes, cut into quarters
   6 slices bacon, cooked and crumbled
   Crushed red pepper, optional
   1 bunch watercress
   2 teaspoons Anisette

Directions
   On a floured work surface, roll out the pizza dough with a rolling pin until very thin. Using a 3-inch cookie cutter, cut the dough into 18 rounds. Brush the tops of the dough rounds with oil, salt, and rosemary (and crushed red pepper if using), pressing the herbs down to make sure that they stick. Transfer dough rounds to a baking sheet and, using a fork, pierce the rounds to prevent bubbles.
   Grill it. Heat your gas grill to medium-high. Use tongs and place dough rounds, herb side down, on grates and grill for 1-2 minutes. Brush the top of each pizzetta with oil. Grill about another minute or until

the bottom is crisp and golden brown. Use a metal spatula to return the pizzettas to the baking sheet when cooked. Top each with 2 pieces of cheese and evenly divided portions of tomato and bacon. Add a pinch of the crushed red pepper if desired. Add watercress, along with a few drops of Anisette. Return the pizzettas to the grill and continue to cook until the cheese is melted. Transfer to a platter and serve while still warm.

Bake it. Heat oven to 400 degrees. Follow the exact topping instructions as for outdoor grilling.

SHELLEY SIKORA-HOLMAN

Mini Pizzetas

Chubby Chicken Taquitos with Easy Guacamole

This is a party hit. Just ask my friends who chowed down during a recent pot-luck party. You will agree that serving this delicious finger food to a large crowd is fast, easy and packed with Mexican flavors and spices.

Makes 16 servings

Ingredients
    16 small, 6-8 inch, flour tortillas
    3 cups shredded rotisserie chicken
    3 cups white Mexican or provolone cheese, shredded
    4 tablespoons canned green chiles, chopped
    2 tablespoons pickled jalapenos, chopped
    4 tablespoons onion, finely chopped
    1 cup store-bought hot salsa
    2 cups canola oil
    4 limes, cut into quarter wedges

Directions
    In a medium bowl, combine all ingredients except the tortillas and the limes. Place about 2 tablespoons of mixture in the center of each tortilla, tuck in the sides, and roll up. Secure with toothpicks.
    Heat the oil in the skillet over medium-high heat. Place rolled taquitos into the oil, and fry in batches until golden brown, about 2-3 minutes. Serve immediately with a side of limes and guacamole (recipe follows).

SHELLEY SIKORA-HOLMAN

Easy Guacamole

Ingredients
   3-4 large ripe avocados
   2 tablespoon lime juice
   2 large plum or Roma tomato, coarsely chopped
   2 tablespoon fresh cilantro, chopped
   1/2 teaspoon sea salt
   Dash crushed red pepper flakes

Directions
   Cut avocado in half lengthwise, and remove the pit. Twist halves in opposite directions to separate and remove the pit. Scoop out the avocado flesh with a spoon, and put into a medium bowl. Coarsely mash avocados with fork. Stir in lime juice, tomato, cilantro, salt, and red pepper until combined. Refrigerate until ready to use.

Puff 'N Pigs With Apricot Mustard

When my daughter got married a few years ago, she asked if I would cater her wedding rehearsal dinner. She wanted it to be casual with a western feel that only happens in Arizona. So we decided that one of the appetizers would be this remake of the old pigs in the blanket. It's quick to make and has a modern twist to an old favorite.

Makes 60 appetizers

Ingredients
    1/2 cup chopped scallions
    1 tablespoon minced garlic
    1 tablespoon extra-virgin olive oil
    8 cups spinach, coarsely chopped
    1 1/2 teaspoon Tabasco
    1/8 teaspoon sea salt
    1/8 teaspoon fresh ground black pepper
    1 package puff pastry, 2 sheets, thawed
    1 large egg, beaten with 1 tablespoon water for egg wash
    1 pound Prosciutto ham

For Mustard
    1 cup apricot preserves
    3/4 cup Dijon mustard
    3 tablespoon honey
    1/2 teaspoon crushed red pepper flakes

Directions
    Preheat oven to 400 degrees. Line 2 baking sheets with parchment paper.

SHELLEY SIKORA-HOLMAN

In a large skillet over medium heat, cook scallions and garlic in oil for about 5 minutes. Stir in spinach and sauté until it wilts and is soft for about 10 minutes. Stir in Tabasco and salt and pepper, and then remove from heat.

Roll out puff pastry on a lightly floured surface, and then slice each sheet into thirds and brush with egg wash.

Layer each third sheet with Prosciutto, and divide spinach mixture equally. Roll each into a log shape, and pinch together the edges to seal them. Brush the outside of each roll with the remaining egg wash. Using a serrated knife, slice each roll into 1/2-inch thick pieces and place on baking sheets.

Bake until golden brown, or about 18-20 minutes.

For the mustard, whisk together all ingredients until smooth. Serve on the side as a condiment.

PART THREE

Lavosh, Crackers, and Crostini

For flatbreads with a crunch, enjoy a fresh, crisp Lavosh, cracker or crostini. Crostini translates to "little toasts" and generally refers to small pieces of bread that are baked. So whatever you call these little toasts, they are always delicious when topped with a variety of ingredients, like cheese, vegetables, meat, or seafood.

Rosemary Parmesan Icebox Crackers

I love making my own crackers. It's hard to believe how simple it is to do and how cost effective it is, compared to buying them from the grocery store. These recipes are unique and simply homemade. You'll be pleasantly surprised how fast your guests eat them, so make plenty.

Makes 24 crackers

Ingredients
    1 cup unbleached all-purpose flour
    1 teaspoon sea salt
    1/4 teaspoon white pepper
    2 teaspoons chopped fresh rosemary, plus extra sprigs for garnish
    4 tablespoons very cold unsalted butter, cut into small pieces
    1 cup grated Parmigiano-Reggiano cheese
    1/2 heavy cream
    1 egg white, lightly beaten

Directions
    Combine flour, salt, pepper, and chopped rosemary in the bowl of a food processor. Pulse to combine. Add the butter and pulse until the mixture resembles coarse meal. Add the cheese and pulse twice to combine. With the motor running, pour in the cream, and continue processing until the dough forms.
    Transfer the dough to a lightly floured work surface, and shape into a 2-inch log. Wrap in saran wrap and refrigerate for 24 hours or up to 2 days.
    Preheat oven to 325 degrees. Line a baking sheet with parchment paper. Cut the dough log into 1/4-inch slices and place on the baking sheet. Dip a sprig of rosemary into the egg white, and place it in the center of each cracker slice. Bake until crackers are light golden brown, or about 25-30 minutes. Transfer to a wire rack to cool.

SHELLEY SIKORA-HOLMAN

Variations

Blue Cheese Walnut Icebox Cracker

3 ounces Reyes blue cheese, crumbled

1 teaspoon sea salt

1/2 stick unsalted butter, chilled and cut into pieces

3/4 cup chopped walnuts

1 cup unbleached all-purpose flour

1/4 cup heavy cream

Follow directions for box crackers.

Red Pepper Cheddar Icebox Cracker

1/2 teaspoon crushed red pepper flakes

1 teaspoon sea salt

1/2 unsalted butter, chilled and cut into pieces

1 cup sharp cheddar cheese

3/4 cup unbleached all-purpose flour

1/4 cup heavy cream

Follow directions for box crackers.

Orange Pepper Icebox Cracker

1/4 teaspoon cracked black pepper

1 teaspoon sea salt

1 cup unbleached all-purpose flour

1 teaspoon fresh orange juice plus zest from 1 orange

1 cup shredded Asiago cheese

3 tablespoons heavy cream

Follow directions for box crackers.

Parmesan Cheese Tuiles

Sharp Cheddar Rounds
with Jalapeno Jelly

Here's a wonderful crisp cracker made with everyone's favorite cheese—cheddar, that is served with a very piquant spread for a hot kick to every bite.

Makes 80 cheese rounds

Ingredients

2 cups unbleached all-purpose flour
1 teaspoon sugar
1/4 teaspoon sea salt
1/8 teaspoon cayenne pepper
3-4 tablespoons cold water, 1 tablespoon at a time

1/2 cup unsalted butter, chilled and cut into pieces
1 teaspoon powder sugar
1/4 teaspoon curry powder
2 cups sharp cheddar cheese, shredded
Store-bought jalapeno pepper jelly

Directions

In the bowl of a food processor, combine flour, butter, sugar, powder sugar, salt, curry powder, and cayenne pepper and cheese. Pulse twice to produce a mealy mixture. Add water, and pulse after each tablespoon is added forming a mealy-type dough.

On a lightly floured work surface, knead the dough and shape into a 10-inch log, and wrap in saran wrap. Chill for at least 2 hours or up to 24 hours.

Preheat oven to 400 degrees. Line a baking sheet with parchment paper. Cut logs into 1/4-inch slices and place on the baking sheet. Using a fork, prick each of the rounds. Bake for 8-10 minutes or until cheese rounds are a golden light brown. Cool on a wire rack. Serve the jalapeno pepper jelly on the side as a condiment. Cheese rounds can be frozen in a sealed container for up to 2 months.

Buttery New England Crackers and Mixed Green Salad with Roasted Vegetables

According to the Almanac, both crackers and their predecessors were born in New England. In 1792, John Pearson of Newburyport, Massachusetts, made a cracker-like bread product from just flour and water that he called "pilot bread." An immediate hit with sailors because of its shelf life, it also became known as hardtack or sea biscuit. This recipe is still a hit today!

Makes 40 crackers

For Crackers
    4 cups unbleached all-purpose flour, plus extra for dusting
    1 tablespoon sea salt
    2 teaspoons sugar
    3/4 teaspoon baking powder
    1 stick unsalted butter, chilled and cut into pieces
    1 cup heavy cream plus extra for brushing

Directions
    In the bowl of a food processor, add flour, salt, sugar, and baking powder. Pulse twice. Add butter and pulse until forming a coarse mealy texture. Add cream and pulse until a stiff dough forms. On a lightly floured work surface, knead dough and form into a disk. Cover with plastic wrap and refrigerate for at least 30 minutes.

SHELLEY SIKORA-HOLMAN

Preheat oven to 400 degrees. Line a baking sheet with parchment paper. Roll out the dough on a lightly floured work surface to about 3/8-inch thick. Using a 2-inch biscuit cutter, cut the cracker rounds and place on the prepared baking sheet. Brush the cracker rounds with the cream.

Bake crackers for 15-17 minutes or until a golden brown. Cool on a wire rack.

For the Salad
    4 tablespoons extra-virgin olive oil, divided
    1 package button mushrooms, trimmed and quartered
    1 small red onion, cut in thin slices
    1 medium zucchini, thinly sliced
    2 Roma tomatoes, quartered
    1 cup gruyere cheese, shredded
    1 garlic clove, smashed
    2 tablespoons fresh lemon juice
    3-4 ounces prosciutto
    Salt and pepper to taste
    5 ounces spring mix greens

Directions
    Preheat oven to 450 degrees. In a bowl, toss together 1 tablespoon extra-virgin olive oil, mushroom, onions, zucchini and tomatoes. Place vegetables on a baking sheet, and roast for 15 minutes or until vegetables are soft. Remove and set aside. Place prosciutto on same baking sheet, and bake about 5-6 minutes or until crisp. Remove from oven and set aside.

    Take 3-4 crackers and place on a baking sheet, and top each cracker with a little cheese. Bake until cheese melts and set aside.

    Mash garlic in a mixing bowl. Add 3 tablespoons of extra-virgin olive oil and fresh lemon juice; season with salt and pepper. Toss in roasted vegetables. Break prosciutto into pieces and add to bowl. Add mixed greens and toss until combined. Serve salad with crackers.

Marinated Beef and Crisp Crostini

For me, anything you put on top of crostini is just good. Here is a tender way to prepare steak that's packed with big flavor. Serve this either as an appetizer or a first course prelude to a fabulous dinner.

Makes 6-8 servings

Ingredients
 1 jalapeno pepper, seeded and chopped
 1 garlic clove, minced
 2 tablespoons red miso paste
 1/2 pound beef tenderloin
 1 baguette loaf bread, very thinly sliced, brushed with olive oil
 4 tablespoons extra-virgin olive oil
 Sea salt and fresh ground pepper, to taste
 Fresh ginger thinly peeled for garnish
 White sesame seeds for garnish
 Mascarpone cheese, a dollop on top of each
 Fresh Italian parsley, finely chopped for garnish

Directions
 Mix together jalapeno, garlic, and miso paste. Use a spatula to coat entire surface of tenderloin with the paste mixture. Cover tightly and refrigerate for at least 2 hours.
 Preheat oven to 400 degrees. Place crostini slices on a cookie sheet, and toast in oven until golden brown and set aside.
 Wipe off the miso paste mixture from the beef, and dry completely with a paper towel. Place beef in a lightly oiled cast-iron skillet or grill pan. Cook over medium-high heat for about 5 minutes on each side or until beef is still rare in the center. Let the beef rest for about 10 minutes, and then thinly slice. Roll beef and place on each crostini. Top with ginger, dollop of Mascarpone cheese, sesame seeds, and parsley. Serve warm or cold.

SHELLEY SIKORA-HOLMAN

Citrus-Basil Shortbread Coins

These may be tiny, but they are big in flavor. But I must warn you. These little bites are very addicting to all who partake.

Makes 16 cookies

Ingredients
  1 cup unbleached all-purpose flour
  1/2 cup powdered sugar, plus extra for dusting
  1 stick unsalted butter, chilled and cut into pieces
  2 tablespoon fresh basil leaves
  Juice of 1 small lemon, plus zest
  Zest from 1 lime
  Zest from 1 orange
  1/4 teaspoon sea salt

Directions
  Preheat oven to 375 degrees. In the bowl of a food processor, place flour, powdered sugar, butter, basil, lemon juice, all 3 zests, and salt. Pulse until a mealy but moist dough forms. Use a tablespoon to scoop dough and, using hands, form a ball into 16 equal pieces. Place dough balls on a baking sheet that has been covered with parchment paper. Lightly dust the bottom of a measuring cup with the powdered sugar, and use cup to press down the dough balls into 2-inch shortbread buttons. Bake for 12-15 minutes or until edges are a light golden brown.
  Optional: Sprinkle tops of baked shortbread coins with dusting sugar.

Grilled Japanese Rice Bread with Wasabi Dip

I can't be the only one who always has leftover rice when I make it at home. I get tired of the usual rice pudding or turning it into fried rice. In Japan, rice is their main staple and this is a great way to use leftover rice. Make bread! This is actually a fun and delicious recipe.

Makes 8 cakes

Ingredients
    For Cakes
    1 cup dry basmati rice
    1/3 cup frozen Edamame, shelled, thawed, and chopped
    For Sauce
    1/4 cup low-sodium soy sauce
    1/4 cup mirin
    1 tablespoon prepared wasabi

Directions
    Preheat outdoor grill to medium-high. Brush grill grate with oil.
    To make cakes, cook rice according to package directions. When done, gently stir in edamame and set aside.
    Transfer 1/4 cup cooked rice to a plastic bag, form into a ball, and push into corner of bag. Shape rice ball into a wide triangle; repeat with rice to form 7 more triangles.
    Heat large skillet or grill pan on medium heat. Lightly coat with olive oil, and add cakes. Grill about 2 minutes per side or until grill marks appear. Dip cakes in sauce, and then grill one more minute on each side to set sauce and remove to serve.
    Serve with side of the Wasabi dip.

SHELLEY SIKORA-HOLMAN

For the Dip

Combine soy sauce and mirin in a small saucepan over high heat, and reduce by one third. Transfer sauce to a bowl and whisk in wasabi until dissolved.

Vegetarian Tomato Soup with Cheese Shortbread Coins

Similar to its cousin shortbread cookies, this savory cheese version of shortbread is great when served with any soup or when served with other crackers, dips and spreads.

Makes 6 servings

Ingredients
For shortbread coins
    1 1/2 cups unbleached all-purpose flour
    1 1/2 cups grated sharp Cheddar cheese
    1 teaspoon dried thyme
    Zest of 1 lemon
    1 teaspoon sea salt
    1 1/2 sticks unsalted butter, softened
    2 large egg yolks

For Tomato Soup
    1 teaspoon vegetable oil
    1 cup finely minced onion
    1/2 cup chopped carrots
    1/4 cup chopped celery
    2 cans, 28 ounces, crushed tomatoes
    3 1/2 cups vegetable broth
    1 tablespoon vegetarian Worcestershire sauce
    1 teaspoon sea salt

SHELLEY SIKORA-HOLMAN

1/2 teaspoon dried thyme
1/2 teaspoon fresh ground black pepper
1/2 cup heavy cream
Optional: 4 drops Tabasco sauce for a kick

Directions

To make shortbread coins, combine flour, cheese, thyme, lemon zest, and salt in the bowl of a standing electric mixer fitted with a paddle. Combine at medium speed. Add the butter and egg yolks. Beat at medium speed until a mealy crumb-like and moist dough forms. On a lightly floured work space, knead the dough and shape into a 2-inch log, and wrap in plastic wrap. Refrigerate for at least 30 minutes.

Preheat the oven to 325 degrees and line two baking sheets with parchment paper. Cut the logs into 1/4- inch slices and place on prepared baking sheets. Bake for 15 minutes or until a very light golden brown. Let cool on baking sheets until ready to use. Shortbread coins can be stored in a sealed container for 3 days.

For the Tomato Soup

In a large covered pot pan over medium heat, heat the oil and sauté onion and garlic until tender. Add carrots and celery. Cook for 10 minutes or until tender, stirring often. Stir in tomatoes, broth, Worcestershire sauce, salt and pepper, thyme, and optional hot pepper sauce. Reduce heat to low. Cover and simmer 25 minutes, stirring frequently. Puree with a handheld immersion blender until smooth. Whisk in heavy cream. Serve with the Cheddar coins.

Sesame Cheese Sables

Buttery, crumbly, and cheesy, these crackers are great with drinks and go especially well with a glass of chilled white wine and off-dry sparkling wines. The dough keeps for two days in the fridge, and for months in the freezer (thaw it in the fridge before using).

Makes 4 dozen hexagons

Ingredients

2 cups unbleached all-purpose flour
1/8 teaspoon cayenne pepper
1 3/4 stick unsalted butter, chilled and cut into pieces
1 1/2 cups freshly grated sharp Cheddar cheese
1/2 cup finely chopped walnuts (optional)
1 large egg yolk, mixed with a pinch of paprika
    and 1/4 teaspoon water, for a glaze

1 teaspoon sea salt
1/8 teaspoon baking powder
1/2 cup freshly grated Asagio cheese
1 large egg, lightly beaten
1/2 cup sesame seeds to sprinkle on top

Directions

Preheat oven to 400

In the bowl of a food processor, combine flour, salt, cayenne, and baking powder, and pulse twice. Add butter, a few pieces at a time, and pulse after each is added. Add the cheese and pulse. Add the egg and pulse until the mixture forms coarse dough. On a lightly floured work surface, knead the dough while adding the nuts. Shape the dough into a disk, wrap in plastic wrap, and refrigerate for at least 1 hour.

On a lightly floured work surface, use a rolling pin to roll the dough about 1/4 -inch thick. Cut out using a hexagon cookie cutter or a shape of your choice. Place cheese sables on a baking sheet lined with parchment paper. Brush on the glaze, and sprinkle with sesame seeds.

Bake until golden brown, about 15 minutes. Let cool on a wire rack. Can be stored in a sealed container for two days.

SHELLEY SIKORA-HOLMAN

Open-Faced Smoked Salmon and Avocado Toasts

There are so many ways you can use breads as a platform to host your favorite toppings. This variation offers a rich way to make a last-minute, elegant appetizer that is guaranteed to impress.

Makes 10 servings

Ingredients
    2-3 firm, ripe avocados, chopped
    1 shallot, minced
    3 tablespoons fresh chives, chopped, plus extra for garnish
    1 tablespoon fresh lemon juice, plus zest from 1 lemon
    1 tablespoon capers, drained
    1 teaspoon jalapeno, finely chopped
    1 teaspoon sea salt
    Fresh ground black pepper to taste
    4 tablespoon extra-virgin olive oil
    1/2 teaspoon coriander seed, coarsely ground
    1/2 pound smoked salmon, cut into strips
    1/2 loaf French baguette bread, sliced on a diagonal and lightly toasted on both sides
    1 medium clove garlic, halved

Directions
    In a medium bowl, gently mix the avocado, shallot, chopped chives, lemon juice, zest, capers, and jalapeno. Season with salt and pepper. In another bowl, mix together the oil and coriander, and toss the salmon with the oil mixture. Rub the toasts lightly with the cut sides of the garlic cloves. Portion the avocado mixture onto the toasts. Pile the salmon strips on top. Garnish with the chives. Serve immediately to make sure toasts remain crisp.

Open Face Tacos

Shattered Lemon Crackers

Mirror, mirror on the wall, who's my favorite cracker of all? It's all about the presentation in this rustic style of serving crackers. Their unique form and shape they take is a great way to use you're your creative endeavors by simply shattering these tasty and crisp bites.

Serves 12

Ingredients
   1 1/2 cups unbleached all-purpose flour
   1 1/2 cups cornmeal
   3 teaspoons fresh rosemary, finely chopped
   1 teaspoon baking powder
   1 teaspoon sea salt
   1 stick unsalted butter, softened
   1 cup sugar
   3 large eggs, plus 2 egg whites lightly beaten with a 1 teaspoon of water, for egg wash
   Zest of two large lemons
   1/2 teaspoon lemon flavoring
   1 cup blanched slivered almonds, finely chopped

Directions
   Preheat oven to 350 degrees. In a medium bowl, combine flour, cornmeal, rosemary, baking powder, and salt. In a standing mixer, beat butter and sugar until combined. Add eggs, lemon flavoring, and zest. Gradually add the flour, and beat until combined. Divide dough in half and place on a silicon liner or parchment paper. Using a rolling pin, roll each half out separately to a 1/4-inch flat single sheet. Brush dough with egg wash; sprinkle with almonds. Bake for 20-22 minutes or until golden brown. Let cool on a wire rack. Break into uneven, jagged pieces and serve.

PART FOUR

Wraps and Sandwiches

These wraps and sandwiches travel the globe with ease, proving that most every culture and its cuisine can be wrapped or sandwiched in a flatbread. In the mood for Jamaican? Try the jerk pork with lime mayo and banana salsa. Latin? Try the grilled baby veggies with roasted poblano cream or the halibut and chimichurri tacos with black bean and corn salsa.

Grilled Baby Vegetables with Roasted Poblano Cream Sauce

This dish was inspired by my friends at a local organic food farm here in Arizona. Nothing is greater than making a fresh and healthy meal for your family. Here we use the smallest and tenderest of vegetables, picked in the infant stages of growth.

Makes 4 servings

Ingredients
    4 to 5 bunches of mixed baby vegetables like carrots, broccoli, corn, etc.
    1/4 cup extra-virgin olive oil
    1 tablespoon minced garlic
    12 ounces (about 6-8) fresh poblano chiles
    1/4 cup sour cream
    1 1/2 teaspoon ground cumin
    1/4 cup chopped cilantro
    1 teaspoon sea salt
    1 teaspoon fresh ground black pepper
    Optional: Dash of Tabasco sauce
    Four 10-inch flour tortillas
    Extra-virgin olive oil for brushing

Directions
    To make vegetables, bring a large saucepan of salted water to a boil. Add vegetables and cook until crisp and tender, or about 35 minutes. Drain and pat dry.

SHELLEY SIKORA-HOLMAN

Preheat outdoor grill or broiler on medium high heat. Brush vegetables with the oil and mix in the garlic. Place in grill basket, and grill or broil inside on a large baking sheet until slightly charred, stirring frequently. Season with salt and pepper.

For Cream Sauce

Heat outdoor grill or inside gas flame on high. Roast poblanos directly over a gas flame or under the stove's broiler. Turn until charred on all sides. Place in a sealed plastic bag. When cool, peel, seed, and remove the stems. Coarsely chop. Transfer poblanos to a blender. Add sour cream, cumin, cilantro, and salt and pepper. Puree. Season with hot sauce if desired.

To assemble, cut off the top third of each tortilla. Spread about 1 tablespoon of the sauce on each tortilla. Equally divide and arrange the vegetables in a row at the bottom of each tortilla. Tightly roll up each tortilla, tuck in the sides, and secure with toothpicks.

Brush wraps with olive oil, and grill over moderately high heat until slightly charred and crisp all over, about 2-3 minutes. Discard the toothpicks and serve with the extra poblano sauce.

Jamaican Jerk Wraps

Jamaican Jerk Pork with Lime Mayo and Banana Salsa

Jamaican me crazy for this fork-tender pork. Simple and not too spicy, this humble dish is awesome. And by the way, the hidden bonus is the salsa, made Jamaican style.

Makes 8 servings

Ingredients
    1 1/2 to 2-pound pork shoulder roast
    2 tablespoon Jamaican jerk seasoning
    1 cup water
    Zest of 1 lime
    1 tablespoon lime juice
    8 flour tortillas, 10-inches
    1 head Romaine lettuce, washed whole leaves
    1 recipe lime mayo (see below)
    1 recipe banana salsa (see below)

Directions
    Trim the fat from pork and cut to fit into a 4-5 quart slow cooker. Sprinkle jerk seasoning over meat and rub in. Add the water. Cover and cook on high-heat setting for 4-5 hours or until meat is very tender. Transfer meat to a cutting board, and let cool completely. Using two forks, shred meat and discard fat. Place meat in a medium bowl and combine with lime juice and zest. Set aside.

Lime Mayo
    1/2 cup mayonnaise
    1/2 teaspoon honey

1/4 cup finely chopped red onion
1 tablespoon lime juice
1 clove garlic minced

Whisk together all ingredients and refrigerate until ready to use.

For Banana Salsa
    Makes about 1-2 cups
    Combine and whisk together all ingredients.
    1 cup banana, chopped
    1/3 cup raisins
    1cup pineapple chunks
    2 jalapeno chile peppers, seeded and finely chopped
    2 tablespoons lime juice
    2 tablespoons finely chopped red onion
    1 tablespoon Canola oil
    1 tablespoon frozen orange juice concentrate, thawed
    2 teaspoons fresh cilantro, chopped
    1 teaspoon ground coriander
    1 teaspoon honey
    1 teaspoon fresh ginger, grated

To assemble, spread each tortilla with the lime mayo then place a lettuce leaf. Add equal amount of pork, divide to fill 8 tortillas. Roll up each into a wrap. Serve with banana salsa.

SHELLEY SIKORA-HOLMAN

Poncho-Wrapped Jalapeno Dogs with Cinnamon Cranberry Relish

Don't you just love having fun when cooking? This is such a happy inspiration for a great lunch or snack that brings us all the joys of our childhood.

Makes 8 servings

Ingredients
    8 (12-inch) all-beef hot dogs
    16 flour tortillas
    1 1/2 cups honey mustard
    2 jalapeño peppers, seeded and chopped
    1 1/2 cups shredded white and yellow mixed Jack cheese, shredded
    Cooking spray
    Cinnamon-Cranberry Relish (recipe below)

Ingredients for Relish
    2 tablespoons extra-virgin olive oil
    1 pound red onions, thinly sliced
    Pinch of salt
    1/2 pound whole cranberries
    1/2 cup water
    3 tablespoons brown sugar
    2 tablespoons blackberry preserves
    1 cinnamon stick

Directions

Preheat outdoor grill to medium-high heat. Grill dogs, turning occasionally, about 5 minutes. Set aside.

To make relish, heat small saucepan on medium heat. Add oil and when hot, add onions and pinch of salt. Cook until browned and soft, about 20 minutes. Add remaining ingredients and bring to boil. Simmer 10 minutes, until cranberries have popped and liquid thickens, stirring often.

Serve warm or chilled.

To assemble, top each tortilla with honey mustard, jalapeño, and cheese. Take a second tortilla and spread it with the relish, and set a dog at one end. Wrap and roll the ponchos around the dog.

Spray the ponchos with cooking spray and grill for a few minutes until brown and crisp and has brown grill marks. Serve immediately.

SHELLEY SIKORA-HOLMAN

Grilled Balsamic Marinated Flank Steak with Roasted Garlic Aioli

Marinated Flank Steak is tender, delicious, and very simple to prepare. Flank steak is a lean, flat cut of beef that's only tender (but extremely flavorful), when properly marinated. And, it's a steak that is delicious when grilled.

Makes 4 servings

Ingredients
    1 1/2 pound flank steak
    8-10 flour tortillas
    2 tablespoons extra-virgin olive oil
    1 cup red sweet onion, julienned
    1 cup red peppers, julienned
    2 medium tomatoes, diced
    1/4 cup Reyes blue cheese, crumbled
    3 cups arugula, chopped

For Marinade
    1/2 cup balsamic vinegar
    1 tablespoon Dijon mustard
    3/4 cup extra-virgin olive oil
    3 cloves garlic, minced
    1 tablespoon fresh thyme, chopped
    1 tablespoon fresh rosemary, chopped
    1 tablespoon fresh Italian parsley, chopped
    Sea salt and fresh ground pepper
    Roasted-garlic aioli (recipe to follow)

For Roasted-Garlic Aioli:
  2 medium whole garlic heads
  1 tablespoon extra-virgin olive oil
  1 1/2 cups mayonnaise
  2 teaspoon apple-cider vinegar
  1/2 teaspoon fresh ground black pepper
  1/4 teaspoon sea salt
  3 tablespoons fresh chives, chopped

Directions

To make marinade, whisk together all ingredients in a bowl. Reserve 1/4 cup to use in the wrap. Place the steak in a sealable plastic bag and pour in the marinade to coat steak completely. Marinate in the refrigerator for at least 4 hours.

Preheat the grill to medium-high heat. Remove the steak from the marinade, and season with salt and pepper. Discard the used marinade. Grill steak for about 5-6 minutes per side or until medium-rare, or 140 degrees on a meat thermometer. Remove from grill and let rest for about 10 minutes. Cut steak against the grain into thin 1/4-inch slices.

For the wrap, heat olive oil in a medium-sized sauté pan over high heat. Add the onions and peppers. Sauté until soft and onions begin to caramelize. Remove and set aside.

To make garlic aioli, preheat the oven to 400 degrees. Cut off and discard tops of garlic heads, and then brush the exposed garlic cloves with oil. Wrap heads in foil and bake until tender for about 45 minutes. Cool and set aside.

Squeeze garlic from skins into a food processor and puree with mayonnaise, vinegar, pepper, and salt. Transfer aioli to a bowl and stir in chives.

To assemble, heat tortillas over the hot outdoor grill. Stack the tortillas on a plate and place on a cutting board. Spread with the garlic aioli. Divide the steak into four equal amounts, and place in the center of the lower third of the tortilla. Top meat with tomatoes, peppers, and onions and blue cheese. Add the arugula and drizzle some of the reserved marinade. Season with salt and pepper to taste. Roll and wrap the tortilla tightly. Serve warm or cold.

SHELLEY SIKORA-HOLMAN

Halibut and Chimichurri Tacos with Black Bean-Corn Salad

Chimichurri is a simple sauce used for grilled meat. It is originally from Argentina but is also used in Uruguay and in countries as far north as Nicaragua, Colombia, and Mexico. It's kind of a pesto for steak.

Makes 6 Servings

Ingredients
    2 cups fresh Italian parsley, stems removed
    2 tablespoons fresh oregano, stems removed
    3/4 teaspoons ground cumin
    1/4 teaspoons cayenne pepper
    1/2 cup extra-virgin olive oil
    1/4 cup lemon juice
    5 halibut fillets, 4-5 ounces each
    1 teaspoon sea salt
    1/2 teaspoon fresh ground black pepper
    Cooking spray
    12 corn tortillas, 6-inches

Ingredients for Black Bean-Corn Salad
    2 cans, 15 ounces, black beans, drained and rinsed
    1 cup frozen or canned corn, drained
    1 tomato, chopped
    1 red and yellow pepper, seeded and chopped
    1 jalapeño, seeded and finely chopped
    2 tablespoons fresh lime juice

1 tablespoon extra-virgin olive oil
1 teaspoon ground cumin
Pinch sea salt and fresh ground pepper, to taste
1/4 cup fresh cilantro, chopped

Directions

Preheat outdoor grill to high heat. In the bowl of a food processor, combine first 6 ingredients until smooth. Place fish in a shallow baking dish and rub mixture over fish. Cover and refrigerate for 2 hours. Season fish with salt and pepper.

Coat the grill rack with cooking spray. Place fish on grill and cook for about 4 minutes on each side. Remove from grill and break fish into chunks. Heat tortillas on grill about 1 minute per side or until light brown grill marks appear. Divide fish evenly among tortillas and serve.

To make black bean-corn salad, mix first 5 ingredients in a bowl. In a second bowl, whisk together lime juice, oil, and cumin. Drizzle over bean mixture, and season with salt and pepper, and then top with cilantro. Serve cold.

Unwrapped Bread-N-Butter Pickle Chicken

I first tasted this delicious dish as a child. My mother worked for the Vlasic Pickle company in Detroit. But she loved pickles long before she worked for the company as the secretary to their President. When she was small, her mother would send her to the grocery store to buy a jar of pickles. By the time she got home, she had drunk all of the pickle juice from the jar. Makes me pucker just thinking about it.

Makes 4 Servings

Ingredients
    1/2 cup mayonnaise
    3 tablespoons white wine vinegar, divided
    2 1/2 teaspoons fresh ground black pepper, divided
    1/4 teaspoon sea salt, divided
    1 teaspoon fresh lemon juice
    1 cup shredded cabbage
    2 teaspoons bread-and-butter pickle juice
    2 (6 ounce) skinless, boneless chicken breast halves
    4 strips cooked bacon
    Cooking spray
    4 whole wheat tortillas
    4 sandwich-cut bread-and-butter pickles

Directions
    Preheat outdoor grill to medium-high heat.
    In a small bowl combine mayonnaise, 2 tablespoons vinegar, 2 teaspoons salt and pepper, and lemon juice. In another bowl, toss together 1 tablespoon vinegar, cabbage, and pickle juice.

Sprinkle chicken with 1/2 teaspoon pepper and 1/8 teaspoon salt. Place chicken on greased grill rack for about 6 minutes per side or until done. Cool and cut chicken into cubes. Combine chicken with mayonnaise mixture in a medium bowl and toss to coat.

Heat tortillas on grill for about 1 minute per side or until light brown grill marks appear.

Place chicken, cabbage mixture, a slice of bacon, and a pickle in each tortilla.

Serve warm or cold.

SHELLEY SIKORA-HOLMAN

Vegetarian Bean and Sage Pita Burgers with Blueberry Ketchup

So who says you have to be a vegetarian to enjoy meatless burgers? Not I. This is another delicious and healthy alternative to using ground beef in your burgers. And for a special treat, serve it with a side of this yummy fresh berry ketchup.

Makes 6 servings

Ingredients for the Burger
    1 tablespoon extra-virgin olive oil
    1/2 cup chopped onion
    2 cloves garlic, minced
    1/3 cup rolled mother oats
    1/3 cup sliced almonds, toasted
    2 tablespoons cornstarch
    1 1/2 teaspoons fresh sage, chopped
    2 teaspoons Dijon mustard
    1/2 teaspoon sea salt
    1/4 teaspoon fresh ground black pepper
    1/2 teaspoon garlic powder
    1/2 teaspoon onion powder
    2 cans, 15 ounce, black beans, rinsed and drained
    1 large egg, beaten
    1/2 cup sour cream
    2 tablespoons red onion, finely chopped
    2 tablespoons feta goat cheese, crumbled
    3 whole wheat pitas, cut in half

6 green leaf lettuce leaves, whole
6 slices of tomatoes

Directions

In a large skillet, heat 1 teaspoon oil. Add onion and garlic and cook for about 2 minutes or until soft. Remove from heat and pour into the bowl of a food processor. Add oats, almonds, cornstarch, sage, mustard, salt and pepper, garlic and onion powder, beans, and egg. Combine until smooth and set aside.

Wipe skillet with a paper towel and add remaining oil. Spoon bean mixture into a 1/2 cup and carefully remove from cup mold and place into pan. Using a spatula, shape bean burger into a round patty. Repeat with remaining mixture. Fry for about 4 minutes on each side. Remove and set on paper towel to drain.

In a small bowl, combine sour cream, 2 tablespoons of onion and cheese. Spread cream mixture into each pita half. Top with lettuce leaf, tomato slice, and bean patty. Serve warm with a side of the Blueberry Ketchup.

Ingredients for the Blueberry Ketchup (makes 3 cups)
1 1/2 cups fresh blueberries
1 medium shallot, minced
1/2 cup granulated sugar
1/4 cup light brown sugar
1 teaspoon honey
1/2 cup red wine vinegar
2 tablespoons fresh ginger, minced
1 tablespoon lime juice
1/2 teaspoon salt
1/4 teaspoon fresh ground black pepper

Directions

To make ketchup, add all ingredients in a large saucepan over medium-high heat, stirring until sugar dissolves, about 5 minutes. Reduce heat to simmer and cook until blueberries are soft and sauce has thickened, 20-30 minutes. Cover and refrigerate until chilled and thickened, about 6 hours.

Vegetarian & Sage Pita Burgers

Vegetarian Wheat-Wrapped Tempeh Greek Salad

Tempeh is made from cooked and slightly fermented soybeans and formed into a patty, similar to a very firm veggie burger. This is by far my favorite way of eating tempeh. I am craving it right now! You can make it vegan by using vegan tzatziki.

Makes 4 Servings

Ingredients
  2 tablespoons extra-virgin olive oil
  1 package, 8 ounces, tempeh (or tofu), cut into 24 pieces
  1 cup water
  3 tablespoons fresh lemon juice, divided
  3 tablespoons plain low-fat yogurt
  1 1/2 teaspoons dried Italian seasoning, divided
  Zest of 1 lemon
  1/2 teaspoon Spanish paprika
  1/2 teaspoon sea salt
  1 garlic clove, minced
  2 cups baby spinach
  1 cup arugula, chopped
  1 cup grape tomatoes, halved
  1 cup English cucumber, chopped
  1/4 cup feta goat cheese
  1/2 cup Kalamata olives, pitted and chopped
  1/4 teaspoon fresh ground black pepper
  4 whole wheat tortillas, 8 inches

SHELLEY SIKORA-HOLMAN

Directions

In a skillet, heat oil over medium-high heat. Add tempeh and sauté 4 minutes or until light golden brown, stirring frequently. Add water and 2 tablespoons lemon juice. Reduce heat and simmer for 10 minutes and set aside. In a small bowl, combine 2 tablespoons yogurt, 1/2 teaspoon Italian seasoning, zest, paprika, salt, and garlic. In another bowl, combine 1 tablespoon oil, 1 tablespoon lemon juice, 1 teaspoon Italian seasoning, spinach, arugula, tomato, cucumber, and black pepper.

Warm tortillas according to package directions. Spread yogurt mixture over each tortilla and about 3/4 cup spinach mixture and 6 pieces of tempeh. Wrap and roll each filled tortilla, and cut in half on the diagonal. Serve immediately.

Curry Chicken with Homemade Mango Chutney

Chutney in this recipe is a bright accompaniment to both vegetarian and meat dishes. It is also delicious spooned over scrambled eggs and is a fabulous alternative to mayonnaise. Chutney keeps for a week in the refrigerator and can be made any time of year. Tip: Look for frozen mangos in the freezer section of the grocery store when you can't find them fresh.

Makes 6 Servings

Ingredients for Curry Chicken
   1 cup plain fat-free yogurt
   3 tablespoons curry powder
   3 tablespoons lime juice
   4 skinless, boneless chicken breast halves, about 6 ounces each
   Salt and pepper to taste
   Bunch cilantro sprigs
   6 garlic cloves, chopped
   Mango chutney (recipe to follow)
   Cooking spray
   6 whole wheat flatbreads (either made from scratch or store-bought)
   English cucumber, cut into 24 slices
   1 1/2 cups baby arugula
   1 cup red onion, thinly slices

Ingredients for Mango Chutney
   2 cups sugar
   1 cup distilled white vinegar

6 cups mangoes, peeled and chopped

1 medium onion, chopped

1/2 cup golden raisins

14 cup crystallized ginger, finely chopped

1 garlic clove, minced

1 teaspoon whole mustard seeds

1/4 teaspoon red pepper flakes

Directions

For chicken, combine yogurt, curry, and 1 tablespoon lime juice, and place in a large ziplock plastic bag. Pound chicken breasts to about 1-inch thickness and add chicken, cilantro, and garlic to bag. Be sure chicken is covered with marinade mixture. Seal bag and refrigerate for about 2 hours.

Preheat outdoor grill to medium-high heat. Remove chicken from bag and discard marinade. Season chicken with salt and pepper, and grill on an oiled grill rack. Cover and cook for about 4 minutes per side or until chicken is done. Let cool then thinly slice on the diagonal and set aside.

For chutney, combine sugar and vinegar in a saucepan and bring to a boil, stirring until sugar dissolves. Add remaining ingredients and simmer, uncovered, until syrupy and slightly thickened for about 1 hour. Stir frequently.

Cool and pour into jars with sealed lids for storing, or serve when ready to use.

To assemble, place 1/3 cup mango chutney in the center of each flatbread. Divide chicken evenly among the flatbreads, and top each with cucumber, arugula, and onion.

Wrap and roll each tightly, and cut in half diagonally. Serve immediately or refrigerate.

Pappadams with Chutney

Mu Shu-Style Chicken Wraps

Mu shu (also can be spelled Moo shu) is a dish style from Northern China. If you love the popular Chinese dish, moo shu pork, wait until you try this version using chicken and wrapped up to ensure you get all the pleasure of tasting the juices in every bite.

Makes 8 servings

Ingredients
    1 store-bought rotisserie chicken, skin removed and shredded
    2 tablespoons soy sauce
    2 tablespoons water
    2 teaspoons toasted sesame oil
    1/4 teaspoon ground ginger
    8 flour tortillas
    1/2 cup Hoison sauce
    2 cups pre-packaged cabbage slaw mix, with carrots
    2 bunches of green scallions, chopped

Directions
    In a medium pan, sauté chicken, soy sauce, water, oil, and ginger, stirring frequently until combined and hot. Warm tortillas according to package directions. Spread Hoison sauce evenly on tortillas. Use a slotted spoon to add chicken mixture evenly on each tortilla. Top with dry slaw mixture. Wrap and roll each filled tortilla tightly, and cut in half on the diagonal.
    Garnish with scallions and serve.

PART FIVE

Smoked Salmon Tortilla Wraps

Main Course Flatbreads

Flatbreads make an elegant yet simple main course. In this chapter we use seafood, beef, poultry and so much more. The key is a balance of flavors, colors, textures and ingredients with, of course, the flatbread. Many of these recipes have no problem throwing tradition out the kitchen door. Sweet potato, prosciutto, and balsamic onion, anyone?

Fast Flats with Beef Tenderloin, Radicchio, and Whipped Ricotta

This incredibly easy-to-prepare recipe lends itself to endless variations of toppings. You can replace the beef with fish or chicken, and any of your favorite vegetables can be substituted for a great, one-dish lunch or dinner.

Makes 8 Servings

Ingredients
    2 tablespoons balsamic vinegar
    10 garlic cloves, smashed and divided
    1 teaspoon lemon juice
    3/4 cup extra-virgin olive oil, divided for marinade and drizzling
    1 round radicchio, cut into 8 wedges
    1/2 cup fresh basil, leaves
    1/3 pound ricotta cheese
    2 refrigerated store-bought pizza dough, cut in halves
    4 beef tenderloins, 6 ounces
    1/4 cup extra-virgin olive oil for steaks
    Sea salt and fresh ground black pepper, to taste

Directions
    For radicchio, preheat broiler. In a large mixing bowl, whisk together vinegar, garlic, lemon juice, 1/2 cup oil, and 2-3 teaspoons each of salt and pepper and set aside.
    On a baking sheet place cut radicchio, and mix with remaining oil. Broil on the top shelf of oven, turning often until slightly wilted, 4-5 minutes.

Add hot radicchio to marinade and gently toss to coats. Cover bowl and let marinate while grilling steaks.

For flatbread, bake or grill, according to the package directions, and set aside.

For beef, preheat the outdoor grill to medium-high heat. Rub each steak with the oil. Rub each steak with a smashed garlic clove, using 4 cloves. Season with salt and pepper.

Grill to a medium-rare or 140 degrees, about 4-5 minutes per side. When cooked, let rest for about 5 minutes, and then slice against the grain and set aside.

To assemble, place each flatbread on a plate. Divide the radicchio and place on flatbread. Drizzle remaining marinade on top. Add the steak. Scatter basil on top and drizzle each with remaining oil. Serve warm.

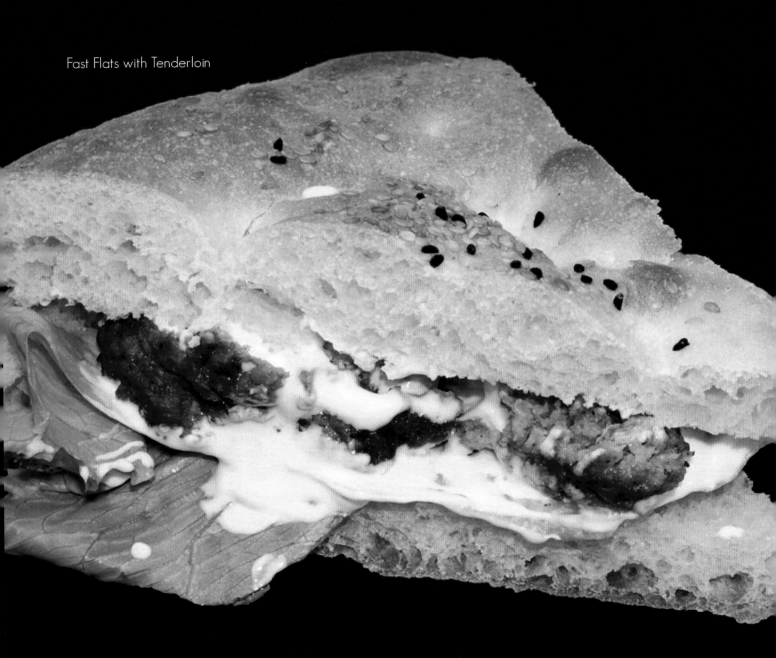

Fast Flats with Tenderloin

Pancetta Wrapped Shrimp and Goat Cheese

Pancetta is Italian bacon that has been cured in salt and spices and then air-dried. So if you are looking for a healthier substitute for bacon, try this recipe. Wrapping the shrimp with the pancetta is easy letting the flavors burst through.

Makes 4 servings

Ingredients
  1 tablespoon extra-virgin olive oil
  1 Vidalia onion, sliced into thing rings
  Salt and pepper to taste
  12 jumbo shrimp, peeled, deveined and tails removed
  12 slices pancetta
  4 pita breads
  3/4 cup or 6 ounces feta cheese crumbles
  Fresh Italian parsley, chopped
  Sea salt and fresh ground black pepper to taste

Directions
  In a sauté pan, heat olive oil over medium heat. Add onions and season with salt and pepper. Cook until onions are soft and caramelized, 15-20 minutes, and set aside.
  Preheat outdoor grill to medium-high heat. Wrap each shrimp in a slice of pancetta. Place shrimp on grill rack and grill for about 5 minutes or until shrimp turn pink and pancetta is crisp. Set aside.
  On each pita bread, divide the cooked onions, and place on one half of the pita bread. Top with cooked shrimp and sprinkle with goat cheese and parsley. Fold pitas in half and return to the grill. Grill each side, for about 2-3 minutes or until goat cheese is softened and grill marks appear on the pita bread. Serve immediately.

Sweet Potato and Prosciutto Pie

My family is from the southernmost part of Sicily, hence a southern contemporary dish using sweet potato and the Italian favorite prosciutto. This recipe will surprise and capture the food enthusiast looking for a something new to try.

Makes 4 servings

Ingredients

1 tablespoon unsalted butter

1 tablespoon extra-virgin olive oil

1 large red onion, thinly sliced

2 tablespoons fresh oregano, chopped

2 tablespoons fresh parsley, chopped

2 tablespoons water

1/2 cup balsamic vinegar, divided

Sea salt and fresh ground black pepper to taste

2 cups cooked, mashed sweet potatoes (about 2 medium-size potatoes)

1 store bought refrigerated or recipe made from scratch pizza dough from cookbook recipe

2 cups mozzarella cheese, shredded

6 ounces prosciutto, chopped

Directions

Preheat oven to 450 degrees. Set a pizza stone in the bottom of oven. Stretch the pizza dough to 12-14 inches and place on stone. Par-bake for about 10 minutes, or until crust is half way cooked. Remove from oven.

In a large skillet over medium heat, melt butter and olive oil. Add onions and oregano. Cover and cook until onions are soft, about 5 minutes. Add water to skillet and continue to cook until onions are caramelized, about 10 minutes. Add balsamic vinegar and cook, stirring occasionally or until liquid has evaporated. Season with salt and pepper.

Spread sweet potatoes over the pizza crust. Top with onions, prosciutto, and mozzarella cheese. Return the pizza stone to the oven and bake for about 10 minutes or until cheese has melted and is bubbly. Remove from oven. Sprinkle with fresh parsley and serve.

Rustic Grilled Turkey-Pesto Burgers

The combination of turkey and pesto is a rich and tasty treat to serve as a great lunch or dinner meal. And the bun is homemade from store-bought pizza dough. You can prepare the turkey patties as well as the pesto ahead of time, refrigerate, than just fire up the grill when you are ready to chow down on a truly great burger.

Makes 6-8 servings

Ingredients
   1 pound store-bought refrigerated pizza dough or made-from-scratch pizza dough cookbook recipe

For Basil Pesto
   2 cups firmly packed fresh basil leaves
   3/4 cup Parmesan cheese, grated
   1/4 cup pine nuts
   1/2 cup extra-virgin olive oil
   3 garlic cloves

For Herb Oil
   1/3 cup extra-virgin olive oil
   1 teaspoon garlic, minced
   1 tablespoon fresh basil, chopped
   1 tablespoon fresh oregano, chopped
   1/2 teaspoon red pepper flakes

For Burgers
   1 teaspoon fresh ground black peppercorns
   2 pounds lean ground turkey

2 teaspoons garlic, minced
1 cup tomato-basil feta cheese, crumbled
1 teaspoon crushed red pepper flakes
3/4 cup Italian flavored bread crumbs
1 egg, whisked
Coarse Sea salt
1/2 Salt and fresh ground black pepper

Directions

To prepare basil-pesto, place all ingredients in a blender or food processor. Cover and blend on medium speed for about 3 minutes, scraping sides until smooth. Set aside. Store extra pesto in refrigerator for up to 5 days, or freeze up to one month.

Preheat gas grill to medium-high heat.

To make buns, lightly flour a work surface, and press dough into a 10-inch circle. Cut into 6 equal wedges. Handling as little as possible, press each wedge into a 4-inch round (uneven rounds give the buns a rustic look). Place each round on a floured baking sheet and cover with plastic wrap for 30 minutes.

While buns are rising, prepare herbed oil. In a small saucepan, combine oil, garlic, basil, oregano, red pepper, and black pepper. Heat over medium heat for 10 minutes. Strain into a small bowl to remove solid pieces. Set aside.

Brush grill racks with oil and place dough rounds with a closed lid for 2 minutes. Open lid, and using tongs, carefully turn buns over. Brush buns with a little of the herbed oil then close the lid and cook for about 4-6 more minutes or until buns are light golden brown. Remove buns and keep warm.

For the turkey burgers, combine ground turkey, garlic, cheese and bread crumbs, egg, and salt and pepper in a large bowl. Form 6 patties. Because the buns will have a rustic, irregular shape, the burgers don't have to be perfectly round.

Grill the burgers until no longer pink inside, about 5 minutes a side. Sprinkle with salt and pepper to taste.

To build the burgers: Spread cut sides of buns with basil pesto to taste, and add the burgers. Add condiments of your choice such as tomatoes and lettuce, etc. Add burgers and serve immediately.

Chicken Pesto with Red Grape Flatbread

Smoked Paprika Flank Steak Tacos with Napa Cabbage Slaw

Smoked paprika is a Spanish specialty made by slowly smoking pimenton (a type of pepper from La Vera, in southwestern Spain) over oak. It's got a round, smoky, woodsy, spicy flavor that's completely different from everyday paprika. It comes in three types, each made from a different variety of pimenton: sweet, bittersweet, and hot. You can find it in most grocery stores. This recipe also has "napa" cabbage, which is actually a type of curly leaf cabbage used in Chinese cooking, and can be found at specialty food markets.

Makes 6 servings

Ingredients
    1/3 cup extra-virgin olive oil
    2 tablespoons red wine vinegar
    1/3 cup soy sauce
    1/4 cup honey
    1/2 teaspoon crushed red pepper flakes
    1/2 teaspoon Spanish smoked paprika
    2 garlic cloves, minced
    1 1/2 pounds flank steak, trimmed
    1 teaspoon sea salt
    1/2 teaspoon fresh ground black pepper
    Cooking spray
    12 corn tortillas

Ingredients for Napa Cabbage Slaw
    1 fresh lime, juiced
    3 tablespoons rice vinegar

SHELLEY SIKORA-HOLMAN

2 tablespoons chili oil
1 tablespoon mayonnaise
1 tablespoon soy sauce
3 cups shredded Napa cabbage
1 1/2 cups thinly sliced radishes
1/2 cup diagonally cut green onions
1/3 cup fresh mint, chopped
1/2 teaspoon sea salt
1/4 teaspoon fresh ground black pepper

Directions

Score the surface of the steak with 1/4-inch deep knife cuts, across the grain. In a small mixing bowl, whisk together the first 7 ingredients. Place the steak and marinade in a large freezer bag. Coat the steak well with the marinade then refrigerate for at least 2 hours or overnight.

Preheat the outdoor grill to medium-high heat. Remove steak from bag and discard marinade. Sprinkle steak evenly with salt and pepper. Place on oiled grill rack and grill for 6 minutes on each side or until a desired medium, or 140 degrees in the center. Remove and let rest for 10 minutes. Cut steak diagonally across the grain, into thin slices. Heat tortillas on grill about 1 minute per side or until grill marks appear. Divide steak evenly among the tortillas.

Serve warm with a side of Napa Cabbage Slaw.

To make slaw, whisk together first 5 ingredients in a large bowl. Add cabbage, radishes, and green onions, toss until combined. Sprinkle with mint and salt and pepper. Refrigerate before serving.

Caribbean-Style Chicken Topped with Simple Citrus Jasmine Rice

I am in love with this recipe and think you will be in love with it too. A flavorful combination that uses spices and fresh aromatic citrus is healthy with subtle flavors that will make you smile with every bite.

4 servings

Ingredients
   2 teaspoons Caribbean jerk seasoning, divided
   2 boneless, skinless chicken breasts, cut into strips
   4 teaspoons extra-virgin olive oil
   1 small red onion, cut into thin slices
   1 sweet red pepper, julienned
   4 iceberg lettuce leaves, washed
   1/2 cup mango chutney
   4 flour tortillas
   1/2 cup cream cheese, softened
   Citrus rice (recipe to follow)

Ingredients for Simple Citrus Jasmine Rice
   1 1/2 cups water
   1 cup Jasmine rice
   1 teaspoon chicken bouillon granules
   Zest of 1/2 orange
   Zest of 1/2 lemon
   Splash of Teriyaki sauce

SHELLEY SIKORA-HOLMAN

Directions

Sprinkle 1 teaspoon jerk seasoning over chicken. In a large fry pan, over medium heat, sauté chicken in oil, turning frequently until chicken is cooked, about 5-6 minutes.

To assemble, combine cream cheese with remaining jerk seasoning. Spread over the tortilla. Spread chutney. Layer with lettuce, chicken, onion, and sweet pepper. Wrap and roll tightly, and then serve with rice.

To make rice, bring water to boil in a medium saucepan. Stir in rice and bouillon. Cover and reduce heat to a simmer for 20 minutes or until rice is tender. Add remaining ingredients. Stir to combine. Serve immediately as a side dish.

Brats and Pablano Chile Flatbread

Flatbread is just so versatile! Here we take a traditional Brat and give it a Mex-packed flavor punch that is so worth a try. It will become a favorite recipe for every party or tail-gate event.

Makes 12 servings

Ingredients
   2 large bratwursts
   2 bottles Guinness beer
   1 teaspoon butter, melted
   2 refrigerated pizza dough, 12-inches, store-bought or from scratch
   2 tablespoons extra-virgin olive oil
   1/2 small red onion, sliced thin
   1 tablespoon sugar
   1 Portobello mushroom, stems and gills removed, cut into thin strips
   4 large button or shitake mushrooms, stems removed sliced thin
   1/2 red bell pepper, seeds removed, sliced thin
   1/2 poblano chile, roasted, seeds removed and chopped
   1 tablespoon cilantro, chopped
   2 tablespoons barbecue sauce
   14 cup Dijon mustard
   14 cup feta goat cheese, crumbled
   1/4 cup cheddar cheese, shredded

Directions
   In a large saucepan, simmer brats in beer until cooked through, about 15 minutes. When done, set aside. Preheat outdoor grill to medium-high heat. On a greased grill rack, grill brats until browned. When cool, slice into thin pieces.

SHELLEY SIKORA-HOLMAN

Roll out pizza dough to form 2 pizzas, about 12 inches. Grill one side of the dough and brush butter on grilled side, and remove. Toppings will go on the grilled side and then be returned to the grill for final cooking.

On medium-high, heat a sauté pan and add olive oil. Add onions and sauté until soft, about 5 minutes. Add sugar and continue to cooking onions until caramelized, about 10 minutes. Add mushrooms and cook until browned. Add red pepper and poblano chiles, cooking until soft, about 2-3 minutes. Add brats and cook until hot. Add cilantro, barbecue sauce, and mustard.

Stir until combined.

Spread brat's mixture over the grilled side of the flatbreads. Sprinkle with goat and cheddar cheeses. Return to the grill and finish grilling pizzas until the bottom has grill marks and the cheese is bubbly. Remove from grill and let rest for 1 minute. Cut each flatbread into 6 pieces. Serve immediately.

Baja Shrimp Tacos with Charred Tomato

Baja is the northernmost and westernmost part of Mexico. It's underneath California…so Baja-style cooking is pretty much a mix between Mexican and American/Spanish cooking. Since us Zoni's (as people from Arizona are called in California), leave our state every summer and head for the beaches in Southern California, I fell in love with this style of cooking many years ago. If you've never tried it at home, you are in for a real treat. It's simple, easy and incredibly delicious.

Makes 8 tacos

Ingredients
- 1 pound peeled, deveined, large shrimp, tail removed
- 2 teaspoon Mexican seasoning or chili powder
- 2 teaspoon extra-virgin olive oil
- 3 cups bagged coleslaw mix
- 1/3 cup spicy ranch dressing
- 1/4 cup cilantro, chopped
- 8 soft corn or flour tortilla
- 1 large avocado, peeled and diced
- 1 mango, peeled, and diced (about 1 cup)
- 4 plum tomatoes, cored and charred
- Salsa, sour cream, cilantro sprigs, chopped jalapeno peppers for garnish, optional

Directions
Preheat an outdoor grill to medium-high heat. In a mixing bowl, toss shrimp, Mexican seasoning, and oil. In another bowl, mix together the coleslaw, ranch dressing, and chopped cilantro.

Grill shrimp about 2 minutes, or until shrimp turns pink, with the lid closed. Set aside.

SHELLEY SIKORA-HOLMAN

Warm tortillas by using a heavy skillet to toast them over medium heat until browned. Or wrap a stack of them in parchment-lined foil and warm in a 400 degree oven for 5 minutes.

To char tomatoes, heat a medium skillet over high heat until very hot. Add tomatoes and cook, turning occasionally with tongs until charred on all sides, about 8-10 minutes. Transfer to a plate to cool slightly. Cut the tomatoes in half crosswise; squeeze to discard seeds. Remove cores and chop the remaining pulp and skin.

To assemble, top tortillas with slaw, shrimp, avocado, mango, and charred tomatoes. Serve with side garnishes as desired.

Peachy Chicken and Gorgonzola Flatbread

Summertime means peaches. I sometimes take the grandkids to pick peaches at the local groves, bring them home and then I slice them up and freeze them so we can have peaches all year long.

Makes 4 servings

Ingredients
    4 boneless, skinless chicken breasts
    1/2 teaspoon sea salt
    1/4 teaspoon fresh ground black pepper
    1 teaspoon extra-virgin olive oil, plus 2 teaspoons
    3 shallots, thinly sliced
    1/2 cup dry red wine
    2 firm peaches, unpeeled, thinly sliced
    1/2 cup fresh basil, chopped
    1/3 cup Gorgonzola cheese, crumbled
    1/2 cup Mozzarella cheese, divided
    1/3 cup balsamic vinegar
    1 prebaked or grilled pizza crust, store-bought or from scratch
    Cooking spray

Directions
    Flatten chicken breasts to an even thickness. Season with salt and pepper. Heat a large nonstick skillet over medium heat, and add oil. When oil is hot, add the chicken. Cook 12-14 minutes, turning once, or until chicken is cooked through. Remove and set aside.

SHELLEY SIKORA-HOLMAN

In same skillet add remaining oil and shallots. Sauté until shallots are soft, about 2-3 minutes. Add wine; stir to scrape up any brown bits. Cook and stir 2 minutes until wine reduces slightly. Return chicken to pan, and heat until hot. Remove chicken and put on cutting board to let rest about 5 minutes. Thinly slice chicken on the diagonal and set aside.

Preheat oven to 400 degrees. Place pizza crust on a baking sheet coated with cooking spray. Brush 1 teaspoon olive oil evenly over crust. Top evenly with mozzarella cheese, chicken, Gorgonzola, and peach slices. Top with remaining 1/4 cup of mozzarella. Bake at 400 degrees for 10 minutes or until crust is light golden brown.

Place vinegar in a small saucepan over medium-high heat; cook until reduced, about 5 minutes. Drizzle balsamic reduction evenly over pizza. Cut pizza into 8 wedges. Serve immediately.

Ancho-Chile Spiced Tenderloin with Sweet Onion and Tomato Pesto

There are so many varieties of Chile peppers that are used as staples in most Mexican kitchens—Ancho-Chile's are my favorites. These peppers are a dried deep reddish brown chile pepper about 3 inches wide and 4 inches long with a sweet hot flavor. When fresh they are referred to as poblano. Anchos are flat, wrinkled, and heart shaped. The ancho however, is the sweetest of the dried chiles.

Makes 12 tacos

Ingredients
   3 tablespoons canola oil, divided
   2 tablespoons ancho-chile powder
   2 tablespoons light brown sugar
   2 tablespoons soy sauce
   2 tablespoons fresh lime juice
   2 limes, cut into wedges
   1 1/2 pounds flank steak
   1/2 teaspoon sea salt
   1/4 teaspoon fresh ground black pepper
   1 large red onion, cut into 1/4-inch rounds
   2 tablespoon extra-virgin olive oil
   12 corn tortillas
   1 tomato pesto (recipe to follow)
   Garnish Options: Sour cream, avocado, shredded lettuce, chopped tomatoes, shredded yellow and white
      cheese, etc.

SHELLEY SIKORA-HOLMAN

Directions

In a small bowl, whisk together oil, chile powder, brown sugar, soy sauce, and lime juice. Place steak in a large plastic bag and cover with marinade. Seal bag and toss to coat steak. Refrigerate for 2 hours or overnight.

Preheat outdoor grill to medium high heat

Remove steak from marinade (discard marinade). Season steak with salt and pepper. Grill onions until lightly charred, and set aside. Grill steak to medium-rare (140 degrees Fahrenheit), about 5 minutes per side. Grill onions and brush with olive oil, 2-3 minutes per side.

Transfer steak to a cutting board and let rest for 10 minutes; thinly slice. While the steak is resting prepare the Tomato Pesto (recipe below).

Warm tortillas on grill until light brown grill marks appear. Spread tomato pesto on tortillas.

Top with steak and onions. Serve with your favorite garnishes.

Ingredients for Tomato Pesto

1/2 cup toasted pine nuts
1 cup packed sun-dried tomatoes
1 cup Parmesan cheese
2 tablespoons oregano
2 tablespoons parsley
1 teaspoon lemon juice
2 teaspoons minced garlic
1/2 teaspoon salt and 1/4 teaspoon black pepper
2/3 cup extra-virgin olive oil

Directions

In a food processor combine the first eight ingredients. Process until chopped. Slowly add olive oil and process until well-combined and smooth. Transfer to a small bowl, cover, and set aside until ready to use.

Shrimp and Watercress Salad with Cucumber-Yogurt Soup Served in a Bread Bowl

I recently did a 30-minute live cooking demo on the internet (you can see it on YouTube as well), for foodieslive.com that featured this recipe. It is cleverly simple using few ingredients and just a blender. This recipe is especially refreshing during the hot summer months.

Makes 4 servings

Ingredients for the Salad
    2 cups Romaine lettuce, chopped
    2 large bunches watercress, 4 cups
    1 cup fresh per-cooked snap peas
    1 cup halved, heirloom cherry tomatoes
    1 package (16-20) frozen shrimp, deveined and tails removed, thawed
    Sea salt and fresh ground black pepper to taste
    1/2 cup goat cheese, crumbled for topping

Ingredients for the Dressing
    1 cup plain fat-free yogurt
    1/2 cup seedless cucumber, diced
    1/4 cup red onion, diced
    1 teaspoon fresh lemon juice

Ingredients for the Soup
    1 English cucumber

SHELLEY SIKORA-HOLMAN

1 cup plain low-fat yogurt
1 tablespoon fresh lime juice
1 teaspoon honey
1/2 teaspoon cumin
1/4 teaspoon sea salt
2 tablespoons low-fat milk
1/3 cup fresh mint, chopped
Fresh mint sprigs for garnish

Directions

Mix together salad ingredients, including the shrimp. Season with salt and pepper.

Whisk together dressing and sprinkle on top of salad. Toss to combine. Top salad with feta cheese.

For soup, peel cucumber and cut in half lengthwise. Cut into 1/2-inch thick slices If using a regular cucumber, scoop out seeds and discard. In a blender or food processor, combine cucumber, yogurt, lime juice, honey, cumin, and salt. Cover and blend until smooth. Whisk in milk. Stir in chopped mint. Cover and chill for 2 hours, or up to 24 hours. Garnish with mint sprig.

Note: Serve soup in a fresh-made bread bowl. See recipe pages 38-39.

PART SIX

Global Flatbreads

The French dress up their flatbreads with basil oil and rosemary, Indians with yogurt and poppy seeds, and Greeks with lemon zest and garlic. While the flavors of these flatbreads are authentic and sophisticated, they require no special culinary skills or equipment. A curious cook with a yen for the unusual will have no trouble mastering these culinary landmarks from around the globe.

Ladopsomo Bread

Ladopsomo Bread

Ladopsomo is a type of Greek-fry bread that is light, puffy, and crisp and is an awesome replacement for traditional bread when served with a salad.

Makes 8 flatbreads

Ingredients
    2 envelopes active dry yeast
    1 1/2 teaspoons sugar
    4 1/2 cups bread flour
    1 1/2 teaspoons sea salt
    2 tablespoons extra-virgin olive oil
    Vegetable oil for frying

Directions

In a medium bowl, combine yeast and sugar. Add 1/4 cup warm water, and let stand until frothy and bubbles appear, 5 minutes. Stir in 1/4 of flour and let stand for 30 minutes. This makes dough starter.

In a standing mixer using a dough hook, place remaining 4 cups of flour and salt. Add 1 1/2 cups of warm water, oil, and standing dough starter. Beat at medium speed until a firm but smooth dough forms, 10 minutes. Remove dough and lightly knead together, and then place in a bowl with the olive oil. Turn so dough is covered all over with the olive oil. Cover with plastic wrap and a clean dish towel. Place in a warm, draft-free area for 1 hour.

Punch down the dough, transfer to a lightly floured work surface and divide into 8 pieces. Shape the dough into balls and transfer them to a floured baking sheet and cover with plastic wrap to rest for 30 minutes.

In a large, deep skillet, heat 1-inch of vegetable oil until hot, and then reduce heat to medium-high temperature. Roll out each ball of dough to a 6-8 inch round disc. Working one at a time, fry the bread turning over only once per side, until bread puffs up and is golden brown. Transfer to a paper towel-lined baking sheet. Repeat with the remaining dough balls. Serve warm. Bread can be refrigerated overnight, and then warmed before serving.

Optional: Top with goat cheese crumbles.

SHELLEY SIKORA-HOLMAN

Indian Naan

Breads from East India come in a wide variety of flatbreads and crêpes which are an integral part of Indian cuisine. This bread is so simple to make and can be stuffed with vegetables or eaten plain with just a little butter.

Makes 6-8 breads

Ingredients

4 cups all-purpose flour
1/4 teaspoon baking soda
1 egg, beaten
3 tablespoon butter, or 3 tablespoons ghee, melted
1 cup lukewarm milk (may use less, adding
    gradually for a soft dough)

1 teaspoon baking powder
1 teaspoon salt
6 tablespoon plain yogurt, room temperature
4 tablespoons extra-virgin olive oil, divided
1 tablespoon poppy seeds

Directions

In a medium-size bowl, sift the flour, baking powder, baking soda, and salt together. Stir in egg, yogurt, and 2 tablespoons butter. Gradually add enough milk to make a soft dough. Knead on a lightly floured work surface. Add oil to a bowl and the dough. Turn dough so that it is lightly oiled on all sides. Cover bowl with a damp towel, and place in a warm place to rise for 2 hours.

Preheat oven to 400 degrees.

Knead dough on a lightly floured work surface for 2-3 minutes, or until smooth. Divide dough into 8 pieces. Roll each piece to form a ball and then into oval about 6-8 inches long. Grease a baking sheet with oil, and brush both sides of the rolled out naan with oil. Sprinkle one side with poppy seeds. Place naan on baking sheet. Bake 6-10 minutes until puffy and light golden brown. Serve warm or cold with your favorite Indian or curry dish.

Fast French Fougasse

Fougasse is the French version of the Italian focaccia bread and can be topped with mixed herbs. The flat bread can be slashed to form shapes (a leaf, tree, or wheat stalk), or the slits can be cut to form a lattice, making the bread easy to pull apart. I developed this recipe with my friend who is a French chef-it's easy and very fast to make.

Makes 2 breads

Ingredients
  2 cups warm water
  2 teaspoons dry yeast
  4 cups bread flour
  1 tablespoon sea salt
  1 tablespoon olive oil

Directions
  Olive or basil oil, coarse salt, rosemary or sesame seeds for toppings, optional

In a medium bowl, mix together the water and yeast. Stir in 2 cups flour until the batter is smooth. Add remaining flour and salt, and stir until dough pulls away from the sides of the pan. Cover and refrigerate overnight or let rise until double, about 40 minutes.

If you refrigerate the dough, remove and divide into 2 portions and let rest for 10 minutes. If not, just divide the dough and proceed.

Heat the oven to 475 degrees. The dough will appear wet. Oil 2 baking sheets, or line the sheets with parchment and oil the paper. Scrape the dough onto the baking sheets. Stretch each loaf into a rectangle. Let rise for 15 minutes. Cut 3 large slashes on either side of each loaf. Sprinkle with any of the additional toppings. Place loaves in oven, and immediately reduce heat to 450 degrees.

Using a plant mister, mist the tops of the loaves. Bake until golden and hollow-sounding when tapped. Cool on a rack. Serve warm or cold.

SHELLEY SIKORA-HOLMAN

Fast Fougasse

Traditional Italian Focaccia

This recipe is an old family secret, that my mother (a professional baker) developed. Similar to its French cousin, you will find this humble, soft and tender bread easy to make.

Makes 1 large flatbread

Ingredients
- 1 tablespoon active dry or quick rising yeast
- 1 teaspoon sugar
- 2 cups lukewarm water, 85-95 degrees
- 5 tablespoons extra-virgin olive oil plus extra for bowl and brushing top
- 2 teaspoons salt
- 4 3/4 cups all-purpose flour
- Coarse sea salt for topping
- 2 tablespoons fresh rosemary, chopped; 1 tablespoon coarsely ground black pepper for toppings

Directions

In a large bowl, dissolve yeast and sugar in warm water. Stir in 5 tablespoons oil and add salt. Add 1 cup flour and stir vigorously with a wooden spoon until flour is well incorporated. Beat in enough remaining flour, about 1/2 cup at a time, to form a dough that is soft and sticky but not completely smooth. Oil a large bowl. Scrape dough into bowl and cover with plastic wrap. Let dough rise in a warm, draft-free area until doubled in volume, about 45 minutes.

Lightly oil a 15x10-inch baking sheet. Do not punch down or deflate the dough. Slide it onto prepared baking sheet. Dough will be soft and should slide easily onto pan. Gently pull and stretch dough to almost cover baking sheet. Press fingertips all over dough to form indentations. Brush top with remaining olive oil. Sprinkle salt and/or herbs, if using. Let rise for 15 minutes in a draft-free area.

Preheat oven to 450 degrees. Bake focaccia on center oven rack for 15-20 minutes or until golden brown. Serve warm or cold. Great for dipping with herbed oils.

SHELLEY SIKORA-HOLMAN

Savory 'N Sweet Apple-Bacon Empanadas

An empanada is a stuffed bread or pastry baked or fried in many countries. This recipe is the perfect take along pie because it is easy to eat, making it a great appetizer or picnic treat.

Makes 24 appetizer size servings

Ingredients
- 4 slices bacon, chopped
- 1/2 cup red onion, finely chopped
- 1 large Braeburn or Gala apple, cored, peeled, and chopped
- 1 teaspoon fresh sage, snipped
- 1 teaspoon cinnamon
- 1/4 teaspoon nutmeg
- 1/4 teaspoon, sea salt
- 1/4 teaspoon, fresh ground black pepper
- 1 tablespoon Calvados apple brandy or unsweetened apple juice
- 1/4 cup Sharp cheddar cheese, shredded
- 2 packages frozen puff pastry sheets, thawed (4 sheets)
- 1 egg lightly beaten
- 1 tablespoon water
- 1 7-ounce container crème fraiche
- 3 tablespoons caramel-flavor ice cream topping plus extra for drizzling on top

Directions

Preheat oven to 400 degrees. Line a baking sheet with parchment paper and set aside. In a large skillet, cook bacon until crisp. Remove bacon and drain on paper towels, reserving 1 tablespoon of the drippings from the skillet.

Add onion and apple to the reserved drippings. Cook, stirring frequently until soft, about 5 minutes. Stir in sage, cinnamon, nutmeg, and salt and pepper. Remove from heat, and add the apple brandy or juice until reduced and almost evaporated. Cool slightly then stir in bacon and cheese. Cover and chill up to 24 hours.

On a lightly floured work surface, roll each puff pastry sheet slightly in to a 10-inch square. Using a 3" cooking or biscuit cutter, cut each sheet into six circles. Spoon 1 tablespoon of apple mixture on half of each pastry circle. Fold pastry over filling, and seal edges with a fork. Place empanadas on the prepared baking sheet. In a small bowl whisk together egg and water for an egg wash, and brush tops with egg mixture.

Bake about 15 minutes or until golden brown. Cool on a wire rack.

In a small bowl combine crème fraiche and the 3 tablespoons caramel topping. Drizzle empanadas with caramel topping.

Serve crème fraiche mixture as a side dipping sauce.

Chicken Koftas with Lemon Yogurt

Kofta is a Middle Eastern and Southeast Asian dish made by grinding meat, mixing it with spices, and forming it into balls or cylinders for cooking. In this recipe we are using chicken as a substitute for lamb.

Makes 4 servings

Ingredients

1 1/4 pounds ground chicken
1/2 red bell pepper, diced
1/2 teaspoon cumin
1/2 teaspoon sea salt
1/4 teaspoon fresh ground black pepper
2 tablespoons extra-virgin olive oil
1 cup fat-free plain Greek yogurt
1 teaspoon finely grated lemon zest
2 tablespoons fresh lemon juice
3 medium Roma tomatoes, sliced thin
4 pitas
1/2 cup fresh mint leaves for garnish

1/2 tablespoon fresh parsley, chopped
1/2 clove garlic, minced
1 tablespoon white onion, minced

Directions

In a large bowl, combine first 8 ingredients. Using your hands, form 8 oval patties. Cook the patties in a large skillet over medium-high heat in oil until patties are a nice golden brown on all sides, for about 12 minutes. Drain on paper towels and set aside.

To make the lemon yogurt sauce, mix together the yogurt, lemon zest, and juice.

Divide the patties and tomatoes amongst the pitas, and fold in half. Top with the lemon yogurt sauce and a sprig of mint for garnish. Serve warm.

Lemon Yogurt Dip

Summer Fresh Tomato and Mozzarella Galette

Galette is a general term used in the French cuisine to designate various types of flat, round, or freeform crusty cakes. I am not a precise or must-be-perfect kind of chef/baker, which is why I love making everything in a simple freeform style. This savory galette is beautifully assembled with my favorite twosomes—tomatoes and mozzarella.

Makes 8 servings

Ingredients
    3/4 cup unbleached all-purpose flour
    1/4 cup cornmeal
    3 1/2 tablespoons unsalted butter, chilled and cut into pieces
    3/4 teaspoon sea salt, divided
    3 tablespoons cold ice water
    1 pint Heirloom red and yellow cherry tomatoes, halved
    1/4 teaspoon fresh ground black pepper
    1 cup bocconcini mozzarella balls, halved
    1/4 cup fresh basil leaves, chopped

Directions
    In the bowl of a food processor, combine flour, cornmeal, butter, and 1/2 teaspoon salt until the mixture has a mealy look. With processor on, slowly pour ice water through food chute, and process until combined. Remove mixture onto a lightly floured work surface, and gently knead into a 4-inch circle. Wrap in plastic wrap and refrigerate for 30 minutes.
    Preheat the oven to 425 degrees.

Place the chilled dough onto a lightly floured work surface and roll out to a 13-inch circle. Line a baking sheet with parchment paper. Place dough on baking sheet. Arrange tomatoes cut sides up on top of dough, leaving a border around the circle. Sprinkle with remaining 1/4 teaspoon salt and pepper. Fold edges of dough over all around tomatoes, just barely covering them so that half of the tomato is still visible. Bake for 25 minutes then remove and carefully place the mozzarella over the tomatoes. Baked an additional 5 minutes or until mozzarella is warm and slightly melted. Remove and sprinkle fresh basil on top. Cut into 8 wedges. Serve warm or cold.

SHELLEY SIKORA-HOLMAN

Arepas Reina Pepiada

Arepas were originally made by the indigenous inhabitants of Venezuela and Colombia. These small corn-cakes are sold in Venezuelan restaurants called *areperías* and are stuffed with all kinds of fillings like a sandwich. Now you can try making this at home. It's really quite simple.

Makes 12 appetizer servings

Ingredients

    2 cups precooked (instant) corn flour (not masa harina)
    1 teaspoon sea salt
    2 cups hot water
    2 tablespoons butter, melted
    2 cups Manchego, pecorino or Romano cheese, shredded
    2 tablespoons vegetable oil
    2 cups cooked, shredded rotisserie chicken
    1 fresh avocado, peeled and chopped
    1/3 cup mayonnaise
    1/4 cup green onions, chopped
    1 jalapeno pepper, seeded and finely chopped
    Several dashed of Tabasco sauce
    Fresh cilantro sprigs for garnish

Directions

    In a bowl, combine corn, flour, and salt. Stir in the hot water and melted butter. Add cheese. Cover and let stand for 15 minutes. (The dough should shape easily and not stick to your hands.) Add additional flour or water to adjust consistency.
    For arepas, shape dough into 12 balls. Flatten balls into 2 1/2-inch rounds.

(cont'd)

In a large skillet over medium-high heat, add the oil. Once heated, add the dough rounds and cook for 6-7 minutes, or until a light golden brown, turning once. Remove arepas and drain on a paper towel. When cool enough to handle, make a cut, not all the way through, in the middle of each.

For the filling, combine chicken, avocado, mayonnaise, onions, and jalapeno in a bowl. Add Tabasco to taste. Fill arepas with chicken mixture; add garnish. Serve warm.

SHELLEY SIKORA-HOLMAN

Arepas Reina Pepiada

Brazilian Pasteles with Chicken

Similar to tamales, pasteles are a very popular dish known around the world; and in this recipe it is comparable to an Italian Calzone.

Makes 20 pasteles

Ingredients for the filling
　　3 chicken breast halves, skinless and boneless
　　1 tablespoon chicken bouillon
　　Water
　　1 medium white onion, minced
　　3 green onions, mince both white and green parts
　　2 teaspoon garlic salt
　　1 teaspoon oregano
　　1/2 teaspoon chile powder
　　Juice of 1/2 lime
　　1 tablespoon corn starch
　　2 tablespoons tomato paste
　　4 ounces cream cheese
　　1/2 teaspoon sea salt
　　1/2 teaspoon fresh ground black pepper
　　Vegetable oil for frying

Ingredients for the dough
　　2 cups unbleached all-purpose flour
　　1 1/2 teaspoon salt
　　1/2 teaspoon baking powder
　　2 tablespoons vegetable shortening

　　　SHELLEY SIKORA-HOLMAN

1 egg, beaten
1 tablespoon vinegar
1 tablespoon vodka
3/4 cup warm water

Directions

Place the chicken breasts in a saucepan with the bouillon. Add enough water to cover chicken. Bring to a boil and simmer 5 minutes. Turn off heat and let stand covered for 10 minutes. Remove chicken and set aside, reserving the broth.

To prepare dough, place flour in a large bowl. Add vegetable shortening, salt, baking powder, vinegar, egg, and vodka. In a small bowl combine 1/4 cup of the reserved chicken broth and 3/4 cup hot water. Add water mixture gradually to flour mixture, stirring well. Add enough liquid to form a dough. On a lightly floured work surface, knead dough gently until a soft dough forms, adding more liquid if needed. Dough should not be sticky. Add more flour if need. Cover with plastic wrap in a warm, draft-free place for 10 minutes.

In the bowl of a food processor, finely shred chicken and set aside. Heat 2 tablespoons vegetable oil in a large skillet, and sauté the onions and green onions until soft, about 5 minutes. Add garlic salt, oregano, chile powder, and cornstarch. Stir frequently. Add the tomato paste and 1 cup of the reserved chicken broth, and simmer until mixture starts to thicken slightly, about 5 minutes. Add the shredded chicken and mix well, adding more chicken broth if mixture seems too thick. Remove from heat and stir in the cream cheese and lime juice until well mixed. Season with salt and pepper to taste.

Divide the dough in half, and roll out each half on a lightly floured work surface. Roll out as thinly as possible to form a 9x12-inch rectangle. Cover with plastic wrap and let rest for 10 minutes. Using a pizza cutter, cut dough in half lengthwise then cut each half vertically into 5 pieces, creating 10 rectangles of dough.

Place 1-2 tablespoons of the chicken mixture in the middle of each rectangle of dough. Dip fingers in water, and moisten the edges of the dough. Place another rectangle of dough on top, and press the two pieces of dough together. Pinch the edges together with the tines of a fork to seal tightly, and repeat with each.

Heat 2-3 inches of oil in a large heavy saucepan or use a deep fryer. Heat to 350 degrees. Fry pasteles in batches until golden brown, about 2-3 minutes, turning only once. Drain on paper towels. Serve warm.

Pastel Brazilian

Pappadams with Pineapple Chutney

These delicious East Indian wafers are usually made from lentil flour. Because they are very labor intensive it is much easier to purchase them. When fried they become bubbly and more enlarged; they're quite artistic to look at. I like the tandoori-flavored ones which are beet red in color. Tip: To maintain crispness, pappadams should be served within an hour of being cooked.

Makes 12 pappadams

Ingredients
   12 pappadams in assorted flavors (wafers available in East Indian and specialty stores)
   5 cups vegetable oil

Ingredients for the Pineapple Chutney
   2 cans, 20 ounces each, pineapple chunks, drained
   4 cups white onion, diced
   3 cups packed light brown sugar
   2 cups golden raisins
   2 cups white vinegar
   Zest of two large oranges
   2 teaspoons sea salt
   2 teaspoons mustard seeds
   2 teaspoons ground turmeric
   Zest of a lemon
   2 medium yellow banana peppers, seeded and chopped

Directions
   To make chutney, heat saucepan over medium heat; add first 10 ingredients and mix well. Add peppers. Bring to a boil. Reduce heat and simmer uncovered for 1 to 1 1/2 hours or until chutney reaches desired thickness. Refrigerate. Serve cold as a condiment. Makes 6 cups.

For pappadams, heat 2 inches of oil over medium-high heat, about 365 degrees in a heavy saucepan or deep fryer. Fry in small batches until bubbly, crisp, and golden brown for about 30 seconds. Using tongs, transfer pappadams to paper towels. Pappadams should be served within 1 hour of being cooked. Place on a platter and serve with pineapple chutney.

SHELLEY SIKORA-HOLMAN

Pappadams with Chutney

PART SEVEN

Grilled Outdoor Flatbread Pizza

Griddle Flatbreads and Pizza

The glory of these flatbreads is that they can be made inside or out, grilled in a pan or on a pizza stone over smoking hot coals. Follow the tips for mastering the dough, and then top with a host of traditional favorites, from basil pesto, fennel, to roasted cherry tomatoes. Or go against the grain with a less traditional pie, from spiced ham with pumpkin seed and glazed pineapple or blistered corn and broccoli rabe.

Tips for Artisan-Style Flatbread and Pies

Temperature – Set oven or grill on high as possible for at least an hour before placing the dough. Most professional ovens reach as high as 800 degrees.

Baking Stones – Restaurants cook pizza on stones at the bottom of the oven to allow stones to maintain constant heat to cook quickly and efficiently. The home pizza or baking stone mimics the commercial stones.

Dough – Be careful not to over mix or knead dough. Less is better. When dough is touched and punched, it releases air and causes dough to be tough, not light.

The Patient Rise – The process of letting the yeast "do its thing" requires patience. Dough needs to double in size to create light and flavorful crusts.

Scratch verses Bought – In this cookbook, you have the option of choosing the right crust for you. Don't feel guilty. Buy fresh pizza dough, use canned, or even substitute flour tortillas. The choice is yours.

Shaping the Stretch – Either use a rolling pin for very thin crusts or shape the dough "freestyle" for a rustic, country look.

Steps for Outdoor Grilling

To grill or not to grill. It's your choice. Bake crust in the oven on a stone. Grill indoors on a stove top or outdoors on the grill.

Outdoor grilling adds a hint of smokiness to the crisp crust. To grill, brush stretched dough on one side with a little olive oil, and season with a pinch of coarse salt. Use hands to place the dough, oiled side down, on the grill. Once the dough bubbles on the top side and the bottom is slightly charred, remove and place on a platter. Grilling should take about 2 minutes. Set aside with the charred side up. When ready, place the toppings on the charred side of the dough then return it with the uncooked side down to the grill to finish.

SHELLEY SIKORA-HOLMAN

Steps for Stone-Baking Indoors

Always place stone in a cold oven before turning on the oven to allow the stone to absorb the heat evenly. Placing a cold stone into a hot oven causes the stone to suffer thermal shock, and it can shatter. Once the stone reaches the required temperature, it is far too hot to handle with a conventional oven glove. Use a pizza paddle to remove the stone from the oven. Learn how much cornmeal works for a particular stone. Use too little, and it's hard to get the pizza off the stone.

Also, it's important to season a pizza stone successfully. This simply means allowing the oil to seep into the stone to create a nonstick patina over time. Always place on a heat-resistant surface, such as a tile, when removing. Allow to cool naturally. Cleaning with cold water leads to cracking.

Steps for Stove-Top Pan Grilling

Grill pans combine the best of outdoor grilling and indoor cooking. Grill pans are available in round and square shapes, so pick the shape that suits your needs.

There are two basic varieties: The first is an oblong shape designed to fit over two burners. The other is a smaller pan, with a single handle and a diameter of about 12 inches. Grill pans come with either a cast-iron cooking surface or a nonstick surface. Cast iron is generally the best choice, because its heavy weight allows it to get as hot as an outdoor grill. Nonstick surfaces can be easier to clean, however.

Always season a grill pan. In order to prevent rust and to keep food from sticking, cast-iron pans need to be seasoned before use. To season, pour vegetable oil on a paper towel and rub the paper towel around the pan, leaving a thin layer of oil covering the entire pan. Place the pan in an oven for an hour at 350 degrees. Allow the pan to cool, and it's ready for pizza. Treat the grill pan like an outdoor grill. Brush the griddle lightly with oil before placing the food onto it, and cook using only high heat. Using a grill pan on low or medium heat causes food to stick.

Cooking with a grill pan can generate a good bit of smoke, so make sure to turn on the fume hood and open a window. Clean and store according to manufacturer directions.

Dough for Fire-Grilled Flatbread

The first time I heard of making pizza on a grill all I could think of was, why would anyone want to do that? Now I am hooked. This recipe is fast, easy and foolproof for creating a thin, crisp and flavorful pizza crust every time.

Makes 2 pizza crusts, about 12 inches each

Ingredients
    1 cup lukewarm water, plus extra as needed
    1/4 cup extra-virgin olive oil, plus extra for oiling the bowl
    1 teaspoon sugar or honey
    1 package active dry yeast
    3 cups unbleached all-purpose flour
    1/4 teaspoon kosher salt

Directions
    In a large bowl warmed by rinsing in hot water, combine water, oil, and sugar. Sprinkle the yeast on top, and with a whisk, swirl to combine. Let stand about 5 minutes until mixture becomes foamy and bubbles. In another bowl, combine flour and salt. Slowly pour the flour, 1 cup at a time, into the water mixture until combined. Dough should feel soft, not sticky or stiff. If too stiff, add a little more water; if too sticky, add a little more flour. Continue to mix until dough is elastic. Turn the dough out onto a lightly floured work surface, and knead for about 1 minute, or until dough feels smooth. Do not knead the dough too much, or it becomes tough. Oil a bowl and add dough, turning until well-oiled on all sides. Cover tightly with plastic wrap and place in a warm, draft-free place until doubled in volume or about 1 hour.
    Punch dough down, and then place on a lightly floured work surface and knead lightly for about 1 minute. Divide into two equal-size balls, and proceed with your pizza or flatbread-making.

(cont'd)

Grilling Directions

Preheat gas grill by setting all burners on high and closing the lid. Reduce heat to medium after 10 minutes. If using charcoal, build a fire with briquettes. Once hot and coals ash gray—about 20 minutes—stack coals on one side of grill and place pizza dough on the opposite side to cook indirectly.

Lightly dust a work surface with cornmeal or polenta. Place dough on top of the cornmeal and stretch by hand, or use a rolling pin to make a 12-inch circle, about 1/8-inch thin. Brush both sides generously with olive oil. Lightly spray grill racks with cooking spray. Pick up the dough by the two of the closest corners, and place circle flat on the grill. Close the lid and grill for about 3-4 minutes, or until there are grill marks on the bottom of the dough.

Using tongs, place crust on a wooden pizza peel, or use a rimless baking sheet. Flip the dough to grill-side up. Add the toppings. Return to grill to finish grilling and set aside.

SHELLEY SIKORA-HOLMAN

Fire-Grilled Flatbread Toppings

Anything goes for pizza toppings in these days of gourmet pizza recipes. But there are limits to what you should do. It's not just a matter of *what* to put on your pizza but *how* and *how much*.

Ingredients for 1 flatbread:

- 1/2 bunch asparagus, grilled, 1/4 cup ricotta, zest of 1 lemon

- 12 sun-dried tomatoes, 6 ounces Brie, fresh basil

- 1 cup basil pesto, 1 cup grilled shredded chicken, 1/2 thinly sliced red onion, 1/4 cup grated Parmesan cheese

- 1 cup sliced plum tomatoes, 1/2 cup shredded mozzarella cheese, sliced red and yellow bell peppers

- 1/4 cup enchilada sauce, 1/4 teaspoon chili powder, 1 cup chopped grilled chicken, 1/2 cup frozen or canned corn kernels, 1 cup shredded Monterey Jack cheese

- 1 cup sliced canned beets, 1/2 cup crumbled goat cheese, 1 cup baby arugula

- 1/2 cup marinara, 1/2 pepperoni, cooked sausage, ham, 1 cup shredded mozzarella cheese, 14 cup black olives

- 1/4 cup Thai peanut sauce, 1 cup cooked shrimp, 1/2 cup sliced red bell pepper, 1/2 cup halved cherry tomatoes, 1/2 cup thawed frozen peas, 1 cup grated Parmesan cheese

- 1/2 cup cooked bacon, 12 baby potatoes boiled and sliced, 1/2 cup sour cream, 1/2 cup shredded Gruyere cheese, 1 cup baby spinach

- 1 cup cooked broccoli rabe, 1/2 cup thawed frozen corn, 1 cup diced yellow bell pepper, 1 cup shredded mozzarella cheese

Skillet Flatbread with Blistered Corn and Broccoli Rabe

It's easy to make flatbread in a skillet. Cooking these rustic rounds on the stovetop is fast work, fun to do and gives them a toasty exterior and moist center. You'll want a well-seasoned ovenproof skillet or rimmed pizza pan or fariata pan. Use a 10-inch and the flatbread will be marginally thicker than it would be in a 12-inch pan. Pour enough olive oil into the bottom so it sloshes around just a bit.

Makes 4-6 servings

Ingredients
> 4 tablespoons extra-virgin olive oil, divided
> 1 whole wheat flatbread dough (see recipe page [Note to Layout: Insert page number])
> 2 ears corn, husks removed
> 4 ounces broccoli rabe, cut into pieces
> 1 cup red bell pepper, diced
> 1/2 teaspoon sea salt
> 1/4 teaspoon red pepper flakes
> 1 cup basil pesto
> 1 1/2 cup shredded Mozzarella cheese

Directions
Prepare your homemade wheat dough according to recipe. Preheat outdoor grill to medium-high heat. Brush corn with 2 tablespoons olive oil. And season with salt. Place corn on grill, turning occasionally until brown, about 8 minutes. Let cool. To remove the kernels, cut the kernels from the corn from an upright position, and set aside.

Preheat oven to 400 degrees. Heat a large oven-proof frying pan over medium-high heat. Add 1 tablespoon olive oil to pan.

SHELLEY SIKORA-HOLMAN

Press the dough out with your hands on a lightly floured work surface to about 14 inches round, and then lift the dough and press into the prepared frying pan, to include up the sides of the pan. Bake in the oven for about 5 minutes, or until a light golden brown, then slide onto a baking sheet. Add remaining oil to pan along with the vegetables, salt, and red pepper. Cook over medium-high heat, stirring often until vegetables are soft and light brown. Add the corn to the vegetables then transfer to a bowl until ready to put onto the pizza crust.

Invert pizza back into pan with the brown side up, and lightly press into pan. Spread on the pesto and sprinkle with 1 cup of mozzarella cheese, leaving a small border around the edge. Scatter the vegetables over the cheese, and then top with the rest of the mozzarella cheese.

Bake 15 minutes or until crust is crisp and cheese is melted. Cut into 8 wedges and serve warm.

Nacho Mama's Pizza with Basil Pesto

Here's a twist on the classic pizza. It's the little things that count, so in this case it's a hint of heat.

Makes 8-10 servings

Ingredients
- 1 gallon peanut or vegetable oil
- 1 tablespoon extra-virgin olive oil
- 1 tablespoon unsalted butter
- 1 tablespoon garlic, minced
- 4 teaspoons unbleached all-purpose flour
- 1 cup milk
- 1/2 cup prepared basil pesto
- 1/4 teaspoon sea salt
- 1/8 teaspoon fresh ground black pepper
- 5-6 ounces sliced pepperoni
- 1 cup sliced button mushrooms
- 1/2 cup green chiles, diced
- 1 pound homemade or store bought pizza dough (makes 2)
- 1/2 cup onion, thinly sliced
- 1 cup shredded, sharp cheddar cheese
- 1 cup shredded mozzarella cheese
- 2 cups pizza sauce

Directions

Heat vegetable or peanut oil in a large pot over high heat, about 375 degrees. While oil is heating, prepare pesto by heating olive oil and butter in a saucepan over medium heat. Add garlic and cook 1-2 minutes. Stir in flour and cook for about 1 minute more, stirring frequently. Whisk in milk and simmer until sauce thickens, 3 minutes. Whisk in pesto; season with salt and pepper.

In a large skillet over medium-high heat, add pepperoni until crisp, about 5-6 minutes. Transfer pepperoni to a paper towel to drain. Cook mushrooms in drippings, about 6-8 minutes, until light brown.

Preheat oven on broil and place rack on the highest level.

Roll out pizza dough on a lightly floured work surface to 1/8-inch thin. Cut dough using a pizza cutter into 2-inch squares. Fry dough squares in small batches until golden brown, 2 minutes per batch. Transfer chips to a bowl with a slotted spoon, season, and toss with salt, and then transfer to a clean baking sheet. Top chips with pesto and all ingredients, and top with the cheeses. Broil nachos until cheese melts and is bubbly, about 2 minutes. Serve immediately with pizza sauce as a side condiment.

Spiced Ham and Pumpkin Seed with Glazed Pineapple

Despite its name, Hawaiian pizza is not a Hawaiian invention. Skip the delivery service and make your own Hawaiian pizza just the way you like it, with plenty of cheese and pineapple. Save time with a boxed or premade crust and you can have it ready and on the table in no time. No more wondering if the delivery driver got lost on the way to your house.

Makes 8-10 servings

Ingredients
    1 pound pizza dough from scratch or prepared for 2 pizzas, about 12 inches each
    1 tablespoon pure chile powder
    1 cup pumpkin seeds, chopped
    1 can pineapple chunks, drained or 1-2 cups fresh pineapple, cut into bite-size pieces
    1/4 cup honey
    1 teaspoon Dijon mustard
    1 tablespoon water
    1/8 teaspoon fresh grated ginger
    1/2 pound thick cut slices of glazed ham, cut into chunks
    1/2 red onion, thinly sliced
    1 cup shredded mozzarella cheese
    1/2 cup grated Parmesan cheese
    1/3 cup cornmeal for dusting
    1 teaspoon sea salt
    1 large egg plus 2 tablespoons cold water, and combine for egg wash

SHELLEY SIKORA-HOLMAN

Directions

Preheat oven to 400 degrees. Lightly dust two baking sheets with cornmeal.

On a lightly floured work surface, divide the dough in half. Combine chile powder and pumpkin seeds in a small bowl. Use a rolling pin to roll half of dough into an 1/8-inch thin rough oval, and sprinkle with half of the pumpkin seeds. Use rolling pin to press pumpkin seed mixture into dough, and roll dough out as thin as possible. Brush with egg wash and dust bottom side with cornmeal.

For the glazed pineapple, combine pineapple, honey, mustard, water, and ginger in a saucepan on medium heat and bring to a boil, stirring to prevent any sticking to the pan. Reduce the heat and simmer until thickened, about 2-3 minutes.

To assemble, place ham, onion, pineapple mixture, and cheeses on top of dough. Bake flatbreads until crisp, 10-15 minutes or until cheese is melted and bubbly. Transfer to racks to cook. Cut long, thin irregular wedges about 6x1 inch. Serve warm.

Fennel and Roasted Cherry Tomato Margherita

It is Pizza Margherita, with a different tiara. The original pizza was made in honor of the Queen consort of Italy, Margherita of Savoy. It's toppings are fresh sliced tomatoes, fresh sliced Mozzarella, and fresh basil leaves. It represents the colors of the Italian flag, and I believe it was the first pizza to use cheese, the pizza's we all know and love today.

Makes 4 servings

Ingredients
   1 refrigerated store-bought pizza dough or made-from-scratch cookbook recipe
   2 tablespoons extra-virgin olive oil, divided
   2 pints cherry tomatoes
   1 teaspoon sea salt
   1/2 teaspoon fresh ground black pepper
   12 fresh basil leaves, chopped
   1 garlic clove, minced
   1/2 teaspoon fennel seeds, coarsely crushed
   1/4 teaspoon dried red pepper flakes
   2 fresh mozzarella balls, about 4 ounces, sliced

Directions
   Preheat oven to 400 degrees. Toss tomatoes with olive oil, and place on a sheet pan. Spread into a layer and sprinkle with salt and pepper. Roast 15-20 minutes or until tomatoes are soft. Transfer tomatoes to a platter, and sprinkle with basil leaves and add salt and pepper. Set aside.
   In a bowl, combine garlic, fennel, and red pepper. Using the back of a fork, roughly crush the tomatoes and add to the bowl with the garlic, fennel, and red pepper.

SHELLEY SIKORA-HOLMAN

Stretch the pizza dough on a lightly floured work surface to form a rectangle. Grill one side of the dough on an outdoor grill according to grilling instructions on page [Note to Layout: Insert page number]. Remove and invert so that the grill side is up. Top with the tomato mixture and the mozzarella cheese slices. Return to grill and cook until golden brown and cheese is melted, about 5 minutes. Cut pizza into wedges. Serve warm.

Fennel & Rosted Cherry Tomato Margherita

Mini Honey Wheat Deep-Dish Pizzas with Apples and Proscuitto

Everyone loves pizza, so why not serve it as the perfect finger food at your next party or get together? But make plenty, it will be eaten up and gone before you know it.

Makes 6 servings

Ingredients
   1 package active dry yeast
   1 cup warm water, 100-110 degrees
   1 tablespoon honey
   1 teaspoon sugar
   2 tablespoons extra-virgin olive oil divided, plus extra for muffin pan
   2 cups unbleached all-purpose flour, plus extra for dusting
   3/4 teaspoon sea salt
   Cooking spray
   Coarse sea salt and fresh ground black pepper
   4 cups fresh mache or baby spinach
   1 cup Reyes blue cheese, crumbled
   1 tablespoon fresh thyme, chopped
   2 teaspoon fresh lemon juice
   1/2 teaspoon fresh ground black pepper
   4-5 ounces prosciutto, chopped
   2 Braeburn or Gala apples, cored and thinly sliced

Directions

Combine yeast and water in a small bowl with honey, sugar, and 1 teaspoon olive oil. Whisk together and let stand for 5 minutes or until frothy and bubbly.

Using a standing mixer with a dough hook, gradually add in flour until combined to form soft but not sticky dough. On a lightly floured work surface, knead dough and form a smooth ball. Place dough in an oiled bowl and cover tightly with plastic wrap; store in a warm, draft-free area for 1 hour or until doubled in size.

Preheat oven to 450 degrees.

Turn dough out onto a floured work surface, and cut in 6 pieces. Roll out each piece into 6-inch circles. Lightly oil a standard 6-cup muffin pan. Place dough into each cup, and gently press dough into bottom and side of cup. Sprinkle with salt and pepper. Bake for 12 minutes or until dough is crisp and golden brown. Let cool 10 minutes.

In a bowl whisk together remaining olive oil, thyme, and lemon juice pepper. Toss salad with dressing and sprinkle with cheese, prosciutto, and apples. Toss in the lettuce.

Fill each mini pizza cup with salad mixture. Serve at room temperature.

Artisan Thin Crust Pizza Bianca

A traditional *pizza bianca*, or white pizza, generally has no sauce, just a covering of mozzarella cheese on top of some garlic, olive oil, and herbs with whatever other toppings are involved. If you aren't in to tomatoes, you will love this recipe.

Makes 4 servings

Ingredients
    All-purpose flour for dusting
    1 teaspoon hot water
    1 teaspoon sea salt
    2 tablespoon extra-virgin olive oil, divided plus extra for brushing
    1 pound fresh or frozen pizza dough, not from tube, and thawed
    1/2 cup whole-milk ricotta cheese
    1 garlic clove
    1 1/2 cups mozzarella cheese, shredded
    1/3 cup Parmesan or Pecorino-Roman

Directions
    Preheat oven to 500 degrees.
    Whisk together water, salt, and 1 tablespoon oil. Coat dough lightly with flour, and then stretch into a very thin rectangle, about 12-14 inches long and about 1/8-inch thin.
    Transfer dough to an oiled baking sheet, and continue to stretch dough to cover bottom of pan. Brush oil mixture on top of dough, and dimple with your fingertips.
    In a small bowl, combine ricotta, 1 tablespoon oil, and garlic. Season with salt and pepper. Spread ricotta on dough, leaving a small border. Brush edges with remaining 1 teaspoon olive oil. Top with cheeses. Bake on bottom rack until crust is crisp and brown and cheese is melted, about 10-12 minutes. Cut into wedges. Serve warm.

Roman-Style Square Pizza

I was born a second generation Sicilian-American in Detroit, Michigan. This is a recipe that is dear to my heart. Detroit-style pizza is a style of pizza developed in Detroit. It is a square pizza similar to Sicilian-style pizza that has a thick deep-dish crisp crust and toppings such as pepperoni and olives and is served with the marinara sauce on top. The square shaped pizza is the result of being baked, not in a pizza pan, but an industrial parts tray.

The crust of a Detroit-style pizza is noteworthy because in addition to occasionally being twice-baked, it is usually baked in a well-oiled pan to a chewy medium-well-done state that gives the bottom and edges of the crust a fried/crunchy texture. Some parlors will apply melted butter with a soft brush prior to baking. Now you can make this pizza, without ever leaving your home.

Makes 4-6 servings

Ingredients
    1 1/2 pound Roma tomatoes, chopped
    1 tablespoon extra-virgin olive oil
    Salt and pepper to taste
    Semolina for dusting
    All-purpose flour for dusting
    1 pound store-bought pizza dough, or use our made-from-scratch dough for two pizzas
    1/2 cup Parmesan cheese, grated and divided
    6 ounces fresh mozzarella cheese, thinly sliced and divided
    10-12 fresh basil leaves, chopped

Directions
    Preheat oven to 500 degrees. Position one rack in the lower one-third of the oven and the other rack in the top one-third of the oven. Place a pizza stone on the top rack.

SHELLEY SIKORA-HOLMAN

Scatter tomatoes on a baking sheet with 1 tablespoon oil and toss. Season with salt and pepper. Place on lower rack and roast until tomatoes are soft, about 8 minutes. Let cool and set aside.

Continue to heat pizza stone for at least 30 minutes more.

Sprinkle a pizza peel with semolina. Divide dough in half. On a lightly floured work surface, roll or stretch each into a 12-inch square shape or 13x9inch rectangle, about 1/8-inch thin. Cover and let rest 10 minutes.

Transfer one pizza to the prepared pizza peel. Brush with some olive oil, and sprinkle with half of both cheeses. Top with tomatoes. Season with salt and pepper to taste.

Set front of pizza peel onto the far edge of the pizza stone, and wiggle off the dough. Bake until crust is crisp and light brown, with cheese melted, about 10 minutes. Using the pizza peel, remove the pizza and place on a cutting board. Garnish with fresh basil. Repeat with second pizza dough. Cut into equal square pieces. Serve hot.

Roman Style Flatbread Pizza

Chicken Pesto and Red Grape Flatbread

This recipe is a homerun with a triple of favorite's that everyone in your family will love.

Makes 4 servings

Ingredients

- 1 can, 11 ounces, refrigerated thin-crust pizza dough
- 1/3 cup store bought basil pesto
- 2 cups rotisserie chicken, shredded
- 1/2 cup Parmesan cheese, grated
- 1 cup arugula, washed and chopped
- 1 tablespoon extra-virgin olive oil
- Fresh basil leaves, chopped
- 2 tablespoons extra-virgin olive oil, divided
- 2 cups seedless red grapes, halved
- 1 cup mozzarella cheese, shredded
- 1/2 red onion, thinly sliced
- Salt and pepper to taste
- 1/4 cup slivered almonds

Directions

Preheat oven to 425 degrees. On a lightly floured work surface, stretch or roll out dough to a 12x9-inch rectangle. Brush dough with half of the olive oil. Place oiled side down onto a baking sheet. Brush dough with the rest of the oil. Spread pesto on dough. Top with grapes, chicken, cheese, and onion. Season with salt and pepper. Bake for 12-15 minutes, or follow package directions until crisp and golden brown. Remove from oven and cool on a rack.

In a small bowl, toss together arugula, oil, almonds, and fresh basil leaves. Spread evenly over top of pizza. Cut into wedges. Serve warm.

Phyllo Pizza with Heirloom Tomatoes and Cracklin' Garlic

Not all crusts are created equal. Tender, flaky, buttery melt-in-your-mouth texture is the easy to make pizza.

Makes 4 servings

Ingredients
    6 layers of phyllo dough
    1 stick butter, melted
    1/2 cup firmly packed fresh basil leaves
    1/3 cup extra-virgin olive oil
    1/2 cup canola or vegetable oil
    6 garlic cloves, thinly sliced
    1/2 cup Parmesan cheese, grated
    1/3 cup Pecorino-Roman cheese, shaved
    1 cup mozzarella cheese, shredded
    3 large heirloom tomatoes, thinly sliced
    Sea salt and fresh ground black pepper
    Fresh basil leaves, for garnish

Directions
    Preheat oven to 375 degrees. For dough, butter a baking sheet with a brush. Lay down one layer of dough, and brush with butter. Repeat process until all dough is layered and buttered. Fold in side of rectangle to form a crust.
    For basil oil, bring a small pot of water to boil. Blanch basil in boiling water for 10 seconds. Drain immediately and plunge into ice-water bath. Squeeze dry and add to blender with olive oil. Blend for 20 seconds. Pour basil oil mixture through a fine-meshed sieve. Discard any solids. Set aside basil oil.

SHELLEY SIKORA-HOLMAN

For the cracklin' garlic, heat canola oil in a small saucepan over medium-high heat. Add garlic slices and fry until golden brown, about 2-3 seconds. Remove from heat and drain in a fine-mesh sieve. Transfer garlic to a paper towel to soak up excess oil.

To assemble, place tomatoes in a single layer on top of dough. Season with salt and pepper, and drizzle with basil oil. Top and spread evenly with all three cheeses. Bake for 30 minutes or until phyllo crust is golden brown. Remove from oven, garnish with fresh basil leaves, and slice. Serve warm.

PART EIGHT

Piadina

Calzone and Piadina

Calzone and piadinas are the hot pockets of flatbreads. Flatbread envelopes on the outside, a host of ingredients, from clams, meatballs, turkey sausage, ricotta, mushrooms and more, stuffed inside. Whether covered in sauce or served bare, they combine main course and sides dishes in a single pocket of pleasure.

Calzone

Classic Calzone Crust

This mess-free turnover style pizza originated in Italy, but we are stuffing it with freshness right here at home.

Makes 4 crusts

Ingredients
    2 packages active dry yeast
    1 1/2 cups warm water, 100-110 degrees
    1 teaspoon sugar
    1 1/2 teaspoon sea salt
    4 tablespoon extra-virgin olive oil, divided
    6 1/6 cups bread flour

Directions
    In a mixing bowl, combine yeast and water; whisk together. Let stand until frothy and bubbly, about 5 minutes. Add sugar, salt, and 2 tablespoons of oil. Using a stand mixer with a dough hook, pour in the liquid and gradually add the flour one cup at a time until combined.
    Turn the dough onto a lightly floured work surface and knead the dough until a smooth and soft but not sticky dough forms. Add a little more flour if too sticky or a little more water if too dry until dough feels soft to the touch.
    Place the dough in a bowl, and tightly seal with plastic wrap and store in a warm, draft-free location for 1 hour or until dough has doubled in size. Lightly punch dough down and cut into 2 pieces. Rub some oil on both sides of each piece, and again wrap in plastic wrap in a warm location to rest for 30 minutes.
    Take each dough disc and place on a lightly floured work surface and stretch and roll to form a round shape, about 10 inches.
    Fill with ingredients and bake, as directed in recipes.

SHELLEY SIKORA-HOLMAN

Perfect Piadina Dough

Piadina is a kind of thin flatbread common in Italian cuisine. It is sometimes compared to pita bread or and lavash. Traditionally, this kind of bread is cooked and eaten moments after being retrieved from the griddle and stuffed with sweet or savory fillings. Now you can make it at home with a few simple ingredients.

Makes 4-6 piadinas

Ingredients
- 3 cups unbleached all-purpose flour
- 1 teaspoon sea salt
- 1/2 teaspoon baking powder
- 1/8 teaspoon baking soda
- 3 tablespoons extra-virgin olive oil
- 1 cup ice water

Directions

In a large bowl, combine all dry ingredients. Make a well in the center of the dry mixture, and add oil and water. Slowly incorporate the flour into the liquid until a soft dough forms. Add more water if too dry or more flour if too wet. Cover with plastic wrap, and let rest 30 minutes.

Knead until a smooth dough forms. Cut into 4 dinner-size servings or 6 smaller appetizer side pieces. Roll out to form a thin 6-inch to 8-inch circle, about 1/8-inch thin.

Heat a large skillet with oil over medium-high heat. Brush each dough circle with oil then place in skillet one at a time. Prick the dough with a fork to keep bubbles from forming. When brown on one side, flip over, and oil the other side. Cook until dough is a light golden brown on both sides, and then remove and drain on paper towel. Repeat with the rest of the dough. Piadina should be soft after cooking, which allows them to be folded over like a sandwich.

Piadina

Stuffed Piadina with Garlic Shrimp and Salsa Cruda

This recipe features salsa cruda, which is a quick and fresh Mexican salsa.

Makes 4 servings

Ingredients
  4 grilled or baked piadina flatbreads

Ingredients for Shrimp
  1/3 cup butter
  2 pounds large shrimp, peeled and deveined, tails removed
  4-6 garlic cloves, crushed
  1/3 cup Italian fresh parsley, chopped
  2-3 tablespoons lemon juice
  1/2 teaspoon sea salt
  1/8 teaspoon fresh ground black pepper
  1 lemon, cut into 4 wedges
  Dash of Tabasco, optional

Ingredients for Salsa Cruda
  3 large tomatoes, peeled, cored and chopped
  1 clove garlic
  4 green onions, thinly sliced
  2 tablespoons red onion, diced
  2-3 jalapeno or Serrano chile peppers, seeded and finely chopped
  2 tablespoons fresh cilantro, chopped

1/2 teaspoon sea salt
2 tablespoons lime juice

Directions

In a large skillet, heat butter over medium-high heat until hot. Add the shrimp and garlic. Sauté over medium heat until shrimp turn pink, stirring frequently about 4-5 minutes. Remove from heat and sprinkle in the parsley, lemon juice, and salt and mix until combined. Remove from the pan, drain, and set aside in a covered bowl to keep warm.

To Assemble

Place 1 piadina on a plate. Fill half with the drained shrimp and fold over. Serve with a side of salsa cruda and a lemon wedge.

To make salsa, combine all the ingredients in a blender, and puree until combined. Serve as condiment. Can be made ahead and refrigerated in a covered container for up to 2 days.

SHELLEY SIKORA-HOLMAN

Calzone a la Marinara

Spinach and Turkey Sausage a la Marinara Calzone

Healthy and light this sandwich-style turnover is a satisfying simple meal or snack.

Makes 4 servings

Ingredients
    2 tablespoons extra-virgin olive oil, plus 4 teaspoons for brushing on dough
    4 turkey sausages, sweet or spicy
    4 calzone dough rounds or 1 tube refrigerated pizza crust, cut and rolled into 4 equal dough rounds
    1 cup mozzarella cheese, shredded
    1 cup washed baby spinach leaves
    1/2 cup ricotta cheese
    1/2 teaspoon sea salt
    1/4 teaspoon fresh ground black pepper
    Cooking spray
    1 small jar marinara sauce

Directions
    Preheat oven to 400 degrees.
    In a large skillet, heat olive oil on medium-high heat. Squeeze the turkey sausage meat out of the casings and into the pan, stirring frequently until browned, about 10 minutes.
    Meanwhile take the calzone dough rounds, brush both sides of each dough, and sprinkle with mozzarella cheese, leaving a 1-inch edge all around. Drain the sausage and place in a bowl, add the spinach to the same pan, and cook, stirring over medium heat until spinach is wilted, about 5 minutes. Remove from heat and drain. In a large bowl, combine the sausage and spinach, and stir in the ricotta cheese and salt and pepper. Spread mixture on top of mozzarella cheese.

SHELLEY SIKORA-HOLMAN

Fold dough over in half, pressing the edges together with a fork. If edges are not tightly sealed mixture will come out, so use a little water if necessary to brush around the edges to help seal.

Transfer calzones to an oil baking sheet. Bake for 20-25 minutes or until lightly golden brown. Serve each calzone with a side cup of warm marinara sauce.

Savory Mushroom Calzone

Mushrooms. Do you use fresh or canned and why? Avoid soggy pizza and calzones when using fresh mushrooms. One trick is to cut the mushrooms thinner before cooking them. This allows for less moisture release and also allows the mushroom edges to crisp up a bit too. The other solution is to boil the fresh, sliced (1/8" to 1/4") mushrooms. Then allow to cool in a colander, and squeeze the water out of them before putting them on your pizza. You can also use this method for canned mushrooms. You'd be amazed how much water comes out of them by squeezing them in your hands or wringing them in a cloth towel. The trade-off is taste when using canned versus fresh. However both canned and fresh mushrooms are good.

Makes 4 servings

Ingredients
- 1/2 cup extra-virgin olive oil
- 1 pound mixed mushroom, cleaned and sliced (such as cremini, shitake, or even button)
- 4 garlic clove, peeled and finely sliced
- 4 springs fresh thyme, leaves picked
- 1/4 cup sweet cream butter
- Sea salt and fresh ground black pepper to taste
- 1 cup tomato sauce 1 package spinach leaves, washed and spun dry
- 4 calzone dough rounds from cookbook recipe or 1 tube refrigerated pizza dough, cut and rolled into 4 equal dough rounds
- Flour for dusting
- 2 balls, 4 ounces each, mozzarella, cut into cubes
- 1/4 cup Parmesan cheese, grated
- Cooking spray

Directions
- Preheat oven to 450 degrees.

SHELLEY SIKORA-HOLMAN

Pour olive oil into a hot skillet. Add the mushroom and toss briefly in hot oil before adding the garlic and thyme. Stir to combine and cook until mushrooms are soft. Stir in the butter. Season with salt and pepper to taste. Add tomato sauce to mushrooms. Cook for a few minutes then add the spinach and stir until spinach is wilted. Simmer until thickened then set aside.

To assemble, place calzone dough round on an oiled baking sheet. Equally divide the mushroom mixture, and using a slotted spoon to drain, place the mushrooms on the dough. Placing mixture in bottom half of the dough, sprinkle each with mozzarella and Parmesan cheese. Leaving a 1-inch border around each, fold dough over in half and seal using the tines of a fork. Be sure that the edges are sealed tightly. Use a little water to help seal the edges if necessary.

Bake for 10-15 minutes or until calzones are a light golden brown.

Country Breakfast Piadina with Red-Eye Gravy

I first tried this idea when talking to my friends from Nashville. They'd say, "There is nothing better than to start your day out with some red-eye gravy." I wasn't sure I agreed until I tasted it. So kick off your boots and rest a'spell when eatin' this recipe.

Makes 6 brunch-size servings

Ingredients
    6 grilled or baked Piadina
    1 pound ground pork
    1/2 cup plain breadcrumbs
    1/4 cup white onion, finely chopped
    1 teaspoon light brown sugar, plus 2 tablespoons
    1 1/2 teaspoons ground sage
    1 teaspoon sea salt
    1/2 teaspoon dried thyme, crushed
    1/4 teaspoon cayenne pepper
    1/2 cup dried cherries, chopped
    1 Extra-virgin olive oil
    3/4 cup strong black coffee
    1/2 cup water
    12 large eggs, scrambled

Directions

In a medium bowl, combine pork, breadcrumbs, onion, garlic, 1 teaspoon brown sugar, sage, salt, thyme, and cayenne. Stir in cherries until combined. Using wet hands, shape the sausage mixture into 6 patties. Place patties on a baking sheet, cover with plastic wrap, and refrigerate for 3 hours or overnight.

In a large skillet, heat oil over medium-high heat. Cook patties until browned on each side and cooked through, about 10 minutes. Keep drippings in skillet. Drain patties on paper towel, but keep warm.

For gravy, heat same skillet on medium-high heat. Stir in 2 tablespoons brown sugar, water, and black coffee into the drippings, and bring to a boil. Stir frequently for 2-3 minutes, scraping the sides until gravy is slightly thickened and turns a reddish-brown color.

In a second skillet, heat butter on medium-low heat, and when hot, add eggs and scramble eggs, stirring occasionally. Set aside and keep warm.

To assemble, place piadina on a plate. Place a cooked sausage patty on the lower half of each, top with equal portion of scrambled eggs, and fold over the piadina. Pour hot gravy over top of each and serve.

Tuscan-Inspired Calzone

A Tuscan, six-cheese pizza is made of a six-cheese blend of mozzarella, parmesan, Romano, Asiago, provolone, and Fontina. However I thought I would save the extra inches around my waist and only use two cheeses. But feel free to try all six in your calzone for a gooey, cheesy delight.

Makes 4 servings

Ingredients
    4 tablespoons extra-virgin olive oil, divided, plus extra for drizzling
    4 portabella mushrooms, thinly sliced and cleaned
    3 garlic cloves, minced and divided
    2 tablespoon fresh rosemary, chopped, plus sprigs for garnish
    Sea salt and fresh ground black pepper to taste
    1 box, 10 ounces, frozen spinach, thawed and drained
    1 can, 15 ounces, cannellini beans, drained
    1 ball, 10 ounces, mozzarella cheese, shredded
    1 cup Parmesan cheese, grated
    4 calzone dough rounds from cookbook recipe or 1-pound pizza dough, cut and rolled into 4 dough rounds
    1 can, 15 ounces, pizza sauce, warmed for dipping

Directions
    Preheat oven to 400 degrees.
    Heat sauté pan on medium high heat. Add 2 tablespoons oil, mushrooms, and 2 cloves of garlic. Stirring, cook until mushrooms are soft and light brown or about 10 minutes. Salt and pepper to taste.
    In a large bowl, mash and mix together the beans, spinach, and the remaining garlic.
    On a lightly oiled baking sheet, place each of the calzone dough rounds. Spread the bean mixture of the dough, leaving about 1-inch edge all around. Divide and top with the mushroom mixture, and sprinkle on the cheeses. Fold the dough over and seal the edges by pressing down with the tines of a fork to seal tightly. Brush the tops of the calzones with some of the extra-virgin olive oil. Bake 10-15 minutes or until golden brown. Serve with a side of warm pizza sauce as a condiment.

Baby Clams, Bacon, and Pesto Piadina

If you have heard of "clams casino," this recipe is my version of that popular dish, minus the shells of course.

Makes 4 servings

Ingredients
- 1 tablespoon extra-virgin olive oil
- 3 medium shallots, minced
- 1 red bell pepper, minced
- 1 teaspoon crushed red pepper
- 3 cans, about 8 ounces, baby claims, drained
- 1 cup cooked bacon, finely chopped
- 2 teaspoons white wine vinegar
- 1 cup dried Italian breadcrumbs
- 1 tablespoons Parmesan cheese, grated
- 1/2 cup mozzarella cheese
- 1/2 cup Asiago cheese, grated
- 2 tablespoons fresh chives, chopped
- 2 teaspoons fresh oregano, minced, or 1 teaspoon dried
- 1/2 teaspoon paprika
- Salt and pepper to taste
- 4 piadina dough rounds from cookbook recipe or 1-pound pizza dough, cut and rolled into 4 dough rounds
- 1 jar sun-dried tomato pesto
- 14 cup red onion, finely sliced
- Sea salt and fresh ground black pepper

Directions

In a large skillet over medium-high heat, combine oil, shallots, bell pepper, and red pepper, and cook until shallots are soft, about 2-3 minutes. Add clams and cooked bacon, stirring frequently, until heated through, about 1 minute. Remove from heat and stir in vinegar. Transfer mixture to a large bowl. Add breadcrumbs, cheeses, chives, oregano, paprika, onion, and salt and pepper to taste. Keep warm.

Bake or grill the piadina dough rounds following the recipe directions.

To assemble, place a cooked piadina on a plate. Spread sun-dried tomato pesto on each. Equally divide and place clam mixture on top of the pesto, and fold piadina over. Serve warm.

Meatball-A-Ball

Everyone loves meatballs, and everyone loves bread. So why not put the two together for a fun and delicious appetizer. It's a good "meat-a-ball."

Makes 10-12 servings

Ingredients
    1 calzone dough from cookbook recipe or 1 tube store-bought refrigerated pizza dough
    For Meatballs
    2 tablespoons extra-virgin olive oil
    1 pound lean ground hamburger
    1 tablespoon garlic, minced
    1 tablespoon, dried parsley flakes
    1 tablespoon Parmesan cheese, grated, plus extra for dusting
    1 cup Italian flavored breadcrumbs
    2 eggs
    1/2 tablespoon sea salt
    1/8 tablespoon fresh ground black pepper

For Assembly
    2 sticks string cheese, cut into 10-12 pieces
    1/2 teaspoon Italian dry seasoning
    1/4 teaspoon garlic powder
    1 small jar store-bought marinara

Directions
    To make meatball, mix all ingredients in a large bowl until well combined. Form round balls, about 1-1/2-inch in diameter. In a large skillet, heat oil over medium-high heat. Cook meatballs until cooked through, and brown on all sides, about 4-5 minutes. Remove and drain on paper towel. Set aside.

Preheat oven to 375 degrees.

Prepare dough by placing on a lightly floured work surface. Roll out thin to about 1/4-inch thick, and using a 3-inch cookie cutter, cut 10-12 circles out of the dough.

To assemble, place a meatball in the center of each dough round. If meatballs are too large, cut in half. Add string cheese piece, and wrap dough around each meatball and cheese. Press and roll dough edges to seal completely. Place meatball bubbles in a greased 8- to 9-inch round cake pan.

Mix together Italian seasoning and garlic powder, then sprinkle on top of each meatball bubble.

Bake 20-23 minutes or until golden brown, and dough is cooked through.

Serve with a side of warm marinara as a condiment for dipping.

SHELLEY SIKORA-HOLMAN

Easy Italian Strombolli

Founded in my Italian roots, this recipe is one that everyone will love – you have my guarantee. While there are many different types of meat turnovers the world over, none are quite like the stromboli, somewhat similar to the submarine sandwich and close relative to the calzone.

Makes 6 servings

Ingredients

    2 links Italian sausage, mild or hot
    1 cup onions, thinly sliced
    1 red bell pepper, seeded and thinly sliced
    1 cup sweet banana peppers, chopped
    2 tablespoons garlic, minced
    1 teaspoon Italian seasoning
    1 pound store-bought refrigerated pizza dough
    1/2 pound ham, thinly sliced
    1/4 pound Genoa hard salami, thinly sliced
    1/2 cup black olives, sliced
    2 cups mozzarella cheese, grated
    2 cups provolone cheese, grated
    1 large egg, beaten with 1 tablespoon water for egg wash
    1 cup Parmesan cheese, grated
    Cooking spray

Directions

    Preheat oven to 375 degrees. Heat a large skillet over medium-high heat. Take sausage and press the meat out of the casing, breaking up into crumbles and cooking in skillet until brown and cooked, about 5 minutes. Remove and drain on paper towels and set aside. In same skillet using the sausage drippings, add onions, bell pepper, and sweet peppers, and cook for 4-5 minutes or until softened. Add garlic and Italian seasoning, and cook for 1 minute. Return the sausage and stir to combine, and then remove from heat with a slotted spoon, cool, and set aside.

Cut dough into two pieces. On a lightly floured work surface, roll out one of the halves to a rectangle about 10x12 inches. Spread half of the sausage mixture onto the dough, leaving about a 1-inch border. Top sausage mixture with half of the ham, salami, olives, mozzarella, and provolone cheeses. Using a pastry brush, brush the egg wash on the border of the long end. Roll into a cylinder shape, pinching the ends to seal. Repeat with second half of dough.

Place Stromboli onto an oiled baking sheet and cover with plastic wrap, and let rest for 30 minutes. Brush the top of each Stromboli with the rest of the egg wash. Bake for 20 minutes, and remove from oven. Sprinkle tops with grated Parmesan cheese, and return to the oven for another 5-10 minutes or until golden brown.

Remove from oven. Slice each into 3- to 4-inch thick slices. Serve at room temperature.

SHELLEY SIKORA-HOLMAN

PART NINE

Desserts

Who says Flatbread cannot be dessert? Wait until you taste these recipes! From frozen yogurt sundaes with apple pie topping, to red-hot cinnamon shards with apples, to chocolate French crepes, these desserts will definitely satisfy your sweet tooth.

Sweet Dessert Dough

Sweet dough is used in making many different desserts, like cakes and pies. Here you can enjoy and use this recipe for fruit pizzas and dessert pizzas. The key is to start with simple and easy sweet dough.

Makes 4 Sweet Dessert Flatbreads

Ingredients
   3/4 cup unbleached all-purpose flour
   1/4 teaspoon sea salt
   1 tablespoon sugar
   1/4 warm water, 100 to 110 degrees
   1/2 teaspoon vanilla flavoring
   1/2 tablespoon lemon juice
   2 tablespoons unsalted butter, melted
   1 teaspoon extra-virgin olive oil
   Cooking spray

Directions
   In the bowl of a stand mixer, combine the flour, salt, and sugar. Using a dough hook, beat dough by slowly adding the water, vanilla, lemon juice, and butter. Knead until combined, about 5 minutes. Turn the dough out onto a lightly floured work surface, and knead lightly to form a smooth ball.
   In a bowl add the olive oil then place the dough into the bowl, making sure that the dough is well oiled. Wrap tightly with plastic wrap, and let rise for 30 minutes.
   Turn the dough out onto a lightly floured work surface, and cut into 4 equal pieces. Roll out each into an 8x10-inch circle. In an oiled cast-iron skillet, place on the stove top on medium-high heat. Cook each dough round separately for about 1 minute per side until dough is charred and a light brown. Remove and set aside until ready to use.
   Fill with fresh sliced strawberries, drizzle with chocolate syrup, and top with whipped cream.

SHELLEY SIKORA-HOLMAN

Chocolate Dough

I have a little confession to make. I love chocolate. And, if you haven't already guessed I love pizza and flatbread. So I thought, why not combine the two that will satisfy both your chocolate and pizza cravings.

Makes 4 Chocolate Dessert Flatbreads

Ingredients
   1 cup semi-sweet chocolate chips
   1 teaspoon cocoa
   1/2 cup shortening
   1/2 cup unbleached all-purpose flour
   1/2 cup white sugar
   2 eggs
   1 teaspoon baking powder
   Cooking spray

Directions
   Preheat oven to 375 degrees.
   Melt chocolate chips, cocoa, and shortening in a double boiler. When melted, set aside to cool. Stir in flour, sugar, eggs, and baking powder.
   Turn dough out onto a lightly floured work surface, and knead until a soft dough forms. Add a little water if dough is too dry.
   Divide dough into 4 equal parts. Roll out each into a 6- to 7-inch rounds.
   Place dough rounds, 2 each, on an oiled baking sheet.
   Bake for 15 minutes or until dough is cooked through. Set aside, cool, and cover with plastic wrap until ready to use.
   Fill with your favorite sliced fresh fruits, ice cream and top with nuts.

Chocolate Dough

French Crepe Dough

The wonderful wafer-thin French pancakes called crepes are made with light sauces and fillings; they suit today's passion for healthy fare. The word crêpe refers both to the individual pancake and the filled creation. Fast to assemble and ballooning with a voluptuous variety of savory fillings—fresh vegetables and herbs, seafood, poultry, and meat crêpes can serve as appetizers, first courses, and entrées. Filled with seasonal fruit, soufflés, sauces, sorbets, or ice cream, they become sumptuous desserts.

Makes 12 crepes

Ingredients
   1 cup unbleached all-purpose flour
   1 teaspoon sugar
   1/4 teaspoon sea salt
   1/2 teaspoon vanilla extract
   3 eggs
   2 cups milk
   2 tablespoons butter, melted
   Cooking spray

Directions
   In a mixing bowl sift together flour, sugar, and salt. In another bowl, whisk together eggs and milk. Using a handheld or standing mixer, beat flour mixture into the egg mixture until combined, and then add the butter, stirring until bubbles appear.
   Heat a lightly oiled skillet or fry pan over medium heat. Pour the batter, about 2-3 tablespoons, onto the pan, and move pan around so that batter spreads evenly, covering the whole surface with a thin layer. Cook for about 1 minute then flip over with a metal spatula and cook the other side for about 30 seconds. Repeat the steps until you are out of batter, stacking cooked crepes on a plate until ready to use.

French Crepe Dough

Deep-Fried Banana Rolls

This deep fried recipe for bananas is quiet delectable. It's crispy on the outside and soft and gooey on the inside. The rich creamy deep fried banana is so delicious the mouth-watering taste will have you and your family hooked on them.

Makes 12 servings

Ingredients
  6 very firm small bananas, peeled and cut in half crosswise
  1/4 cup butter, melted
  1/2 cup light brown sugar
  1/2 cup finely chopped nuts
  1 egg white, beaten
  12 eggroll wrappers
  Vegetable oil, for frying
  Powder sugar for dusting

Directions
  Heat about 2 inches of oil in a deep fryer or cast-iron frying pan. Peel and halve bananas. In a bowl combine brown sugar and nuts. On a flat work surface, place down 12 eggroll wrappers, with the diamond shape facing you. Take a banana half and dip it into the butter, and then roll it in the sugar-nut mixture. Place in the center of the wrapper, fold in the sides, and then fold up the bottom. Use fingers to apply the egg white to the top flap, fold down, and then seal it tightly.
  When oil is hot, slowly drop each egg roll 2 at a time into the oil. When the bottom turns golden brown, using tongs, turn over and brown the other side, about 5 minutes total for each.
  Drain on paper towels. Cut in half on the diagonal. Sprinkle with powder sugar, and serve warm.

Deep-fried Banana Rolls

Pear Frangipane Tart
with Pomegranate Sauce

Frangipane, sometimes spelled frangipani, is similar to a pastry cream, and is often called an almond pastry cream. However, frangipane can be any cream or custard-like substance with different nuts. What makes it different from the average pastry cream is that it is often used as a filling in pies and is baked. This results in a very different crusty exterior to pies or tarts, and it is a quite rich and delicious alternative to stand-ard fruit pies. And contrary to popular belief, it does not need to contain almonds. You're going to love this recipe.

Makes 6 tarts

Ingredients
    7 ounce package almond paste (not marzipan)
    1/4 cup powdered sugar
    4 tablespoon butter, melted and divided in half
    2 eggs
    12 sheets frozen phyllo dough, 14x9 inches, thawed
    3 Bartlett or Bosc pears, peeled and thinly sliced
    2 tablespoons sugar
    2 tablespoons apple or pear jelly
    For the pomegranate sauce
    2/3 cup dry red wine
    3/4 cup pomegranate juice
    1/2 cup sugar
    3/4 teaspoon cinnamon
    2 teaspoons orange zest

Directions

Preheat the oven to 375 degrees.

In a food processor, crumble almond paste. Add powdered sugar and half of the butter, and combine until mixed. Add eggs, cover, and process again until smooth. Set aside.

Arrange 1 phyllo sheet on a cutting board, and brush lightly with melted butter. Top with another phyllo sheet, and brush with remaining butter. Fold phyllo stack in half lengthwise to form a 9x7-inch stack. Loosely fold up toward the center to create a 4x5-inch tart shell. Place on a baking sheet lined with parchment paper. Coat shell with cooking spray. Repeat procedure with the remaining phyllo sheets, butter, and cooking spray until you have formed 6 tart shells.

Spread nut mixture into each tart shell. Arrange pear slices over the almond filling, pressing in slightly. Sprinkle with lemon juice then with sugar.

Bake for 20-25 minutes or until phyllo is crisp and light brown.

Place jelly into a small bowl, and microwave for about 20 seconds or until jelly melts. Carefully brush jelly over tarts.

For the pomegranate sauce, combine wine, juice, sugar, cinnamon, and zest in medium saucepan. Cook over medium heat for about 3 minutes or until sugar dissolves. Remove from heat and set aside.

Place tarts on individual plates, and drizzle with pomegranate sauce.

Optional: Top each tart with dollop of mascarpone or a scoop of vanilla ice cream.

Pear Frangipane Tart

Meyer Lemon Curd with Berry Compote

Thought to be a cross between a mandarin and a true lemon, Meyer lemons are rounder, smaller, and have a sweeter juice than the standard variety you'll find in the grocery store. Thanks to Frank N. Meyer, who first discovered this fragrant fruit in 1908 by bringing this citrus fruit from China to California. Because the juice is much sweeter, Meyer lemons make a great cocktail starter. And whatever you do, don't throw away the peels! The zest of the Meyer lemon can be used in everything and are especially great in vinaigrettes and desserts.

Makes 4 piadinas

Ingredients
    1 recipe sweet dough in this chapter

Ingredients for Berry Compote
    3 cups mixed ripe raspberries, blackberries and blueberries, rinsed
    1/2 cup sugar
    1 teaspoon Meyer lemon juice (or regular lemon juice)

Ingredients for Curd
    4 eggs
    4 egg yolks
    1 cup sugar
    1 1/2 cup Meyer lemon juice (or 2/3 cups regular lemon juice)
    Grated zest of 4 Meyer lemons (or 2 small lemons)
    6 ounces unsalted butter, cut into small pieces, at room temperature
    3 tablespoons powdered sugar

SHELLEY SIKORA-HOLMAN

Whipped cream, for garnish
Fresh mint sprigs, for garnish

Directions

In a saucepan over medium heat, make berry compote by combining berries, sugar, and lemon juice. Stir and simmer until sugar dissolves, and berries have released their juices. Continue to simmer, stirring frequently until sauce thickens, about 5 minutes. Remove from heat and transfer to a bowl. Cover and cool or refrigerate.

Bring about 2 inches of water to boil in a saucepan over medium-high heat. Using a metal bowl with a rim so that the bowl will sit on top of the saucepan without the bowl touching the water, whisk together by slowly adding the whole eggs, egg yolks, and sugar. If eggs become too hot, they scramble. If scrambled, discard and start over. Gradually whisk in the lemon juice and zest. Reduce the heat to keep the water at a gently simmer. Continue to whisk egg mixture until it thickens, about 10 minutes. Turn off the heat and whisk in the butter a few pieces at a time. Place a fine meshed sieve over a bowl, and strain the lemon curd filling through the sieve and into the bowl. Let cool.

Place a grilled piadina on a plate, and using a rubber spatula, spoon the lemon curd onto one half of each. Fold over and top with berry compote. Sprinkle each with powdered sugar. Garnish with whipped cream and fresh mint sprigs, and serve.

Frozen Yogurt Sundae with Apple Pie Topping and Sweet Pita Wedges

You are in for a real treat with this twist on an American classic. But instead of a traditional slice of apple pie being topped with ice cream, here we make a sundae and top it with the apple pie crumbles! It's absolutely scrumptious.

Makes 8 servings

Ingredients for Sundae
- 6 tablespoon unsalted butter
- 1 teaspoon all-purpose flour
- 6 large apples, Gala or McIntosh, cored, peeled, and thinly sliced
- Juice of 1 lemon
- 1/4 cup sugar, plus 2 tablespoons
- 1/4 cup brown sugar
- 1/2 teaspoon ground cinnamon
- 1/8 teaspoon ground nutmeg
- 1/2 cup water
- 1/2 gallon vanilla frozen yogurt

Ingredients for Sweet Pita Wedges
- 1 1/2 cups whole milk
- 6 large eggs
- 1/2 sugar
- 2 tablespoons lemon zest
- 1/2 teaspoon ground nutmeg
- 1/8 teaspoon sea salt

SHELLEY SIKORA-HOLMAN

4 whole pitas, cut into quarters
2 tablespoons unsalted butter
Powdered sugar, for dusting

Directions

In a large skillet over medium heat, make sundae by melting butter and stirring in the flour. Pour and mix lemon juice with the apples to keep them from turning brown. Once combined, add the apples to skillet and toss to coat. Add the sugar, brown sugar, cinnamon, and nutmeg, and season lightly with salt. Continue to cook until apples are tender, about 15 minutes. Add 1/2 cup water to the skillet, and bring to a boil. Remove from heat and transfer half of the apples to a blender, and puree until smooth. Pour puree into a bowl and freeze until cold, about 30 minutes. Soften the frozen yogurt slightly, and scoop out and combine with the cold apple puree. Refreeze apple yogurt until firm, about 30 minutes.

To make sweet pita wedges, whisk together milk, eggs, sugar, lemon zest, nutmeg, and salt in shallow, flat bowl. Place cut pitas in dish to soak for about 15 minutes, flipping halfway through.

In a large skillet, melt butter over medium heat. Place pitas from egg mixture, letting excess drip off, into pan, and cook until golden brown on both sides, about 5 minutes per side. Transfer to paper towels and cover to keep warm. Repeat with remaining pits wedges. Dust wedges with powder sugar.

Scoop the frozen yogurt into bowls, and top with sautéed apples. Serve on the side of the sundaes.

Red-Hot Cinnamon Shards
and Apple Piadina

A shard is like a broken piece of glass without the bad luck. But in this instance it is made out of candy. This cinnamon shards are literally "red hot."

Makes 4 dessert piadinas

Ingredients
    1 recipe sweet dough
    3/4 cup red-hot cinnamon candies
    2 tablespoons water
    2 tablespoon light corn syrup
    1 cup sugar
    Powdered sugar, for dusting.
    2 tablespoon firmly packed brown sugar
    2 tablespoon butter
    5 Granny Smith apples, peeled, cored, and thinly sliced
    1/2 cup whipping cream
    1 tablespoon sugar
    1/2 teaspoon vanilla extract
    Cooking spray

Directions
    Preheat oven to 425 degrees.
    To make shards, heat cinnamon candies, water, syrup, and sugar to boiling in a saucepan. Reduce heat and simmer uncovered, stirring frequently until candies are partially melted, about 10 minutes. Pour the mixture into a 15x10x1-inch oiled baking pan. Let stand until completely cooled. Break candy into small

shards by tapping the baking sheet on the counter, or tap surface with a wooden spoon. Sprinkle with powdered sugar.

For apples, heat brown sugar and butter in a large heavy skillet over medium-high heat, stirring frequently until sugar is dissolved. Add apples and cook until apples are tender and crisp, about 4-5 minutes. Remove from heat and keep warm.

For whipped cream, beat cream with sugar and vanilla in a chilled mixing bowl until stiff. Refrigerate until ready to serve.

Place a grilled piadina on a plate. Spread the apples on half of the piadina and fold over. Place a scoop of whipped cream on top, and garnish with a red-hot cinnamon shard.

So-Easy S'mores Pizza

S'More is supposed to be an abbreviation for "some more," which girls used to chant around the campfire. Loretta Scott Crew seems to have been the first to include the recipe in a book, but it is thought that S'Mores originated with the Campfire Girls in the 1920s and were then "discovered" by the Girl Scouts. This recipe rediscovers this old classic that is still a popular favorite to both kids and adults.

Makes 4 pizzas

Ingredients
  1 cup graham crackers, coarsely chopped
  2 tablespoons light brown sugar
  2 tablespoons granulated sugar
  1 tablespoon, butter, softened
  1/4 teaspoon vanilla extract
  1/8 teaspoon sea salt
  1 recipe sweet dough from this chapter
  1 cup semi-sweet chocolate chips
  2 cups mini-marshmallows
  Powdered sugar, for dusting

Directions
  Preheat oven to 400 degrees.
  In a food processor, combine graham crackers, brown sugar, sugar, butter, vanilla, and salt. Pulse to make a fine crumb. Place grilled piadinas on a cookie sheet, and top each with one-fourth of the graham cracker crumbs, chocolate, and marshmallows. Bake 5-6 minutes or until marshmallows and chocolate are melted. Sift powdered sugar on top, and serve immediately.

SHELLEY SIKORA-HOLMAN

Peach Cobbler
with Butter-Crust Cookies

Don't you just love cobblers? Fresh, not too sweet, and simple to make, this recipe is made with cookies.

Makes 6 servings

Ingredients
   1/4 cup butter
   7-8 peaches, peeled and sliced
   1 cup sugar
   2 tablespoon all-purpose flour
   2 tablespoons lemon juice
   1/2 teaspoon ground cinnamon
   1/8 teaspoon ground nutmeg
   1 frozen or refrigerated pie crust
   2 tablespoon butter, melted
   1 tablespoon granulated sugar
   1/2 cup heavy whipping cream
   1 tablespoon sugar
   1/2 teaspoon vanilla extract

Directions
   Preheat oven to 450 degrees.
   Melt butter in a heavy saucepan over medium heat. Add peaches, sugar, flour, lemon juice, and cinnamon and nutmeg. Bring to a boil and reduce heat to simmer for 10 minutes, or until peaches are tender, and set aside but keep warm.

On a lightly floured work surface, roll out pie crust. Using a 3-inch round cookie cutter, cut out 12 circles. Make 4 small holes in the center of each circle, using a toothpick or straw.

Place circles on a parchment-lined baking sheet. Lightly brush each circle with melted butter, and sprinkle with sugar. Bake for 8-10 minutes or until a light golden brown. Remove and cool on a rack.

Beat together heavy whipping cream, sugar, and vanilla in a chilled metal bowl until stiff.

To assemble, place 1 cookie in the bottom of 6 ramekins, 7 ounces each. Spoon in peach mixture, and stick one more cookie upright in the ramekin. Serve with a dollop of whipped cream.

SHELLEY SIKORA-HOLMAN

Ceylon Cinnamon-Orange Churros

This type of cinnamon, known throughout Mexico, has a lighter and finer texture to it the other types. This cinnamon can be easily ground up with a spice grinder and is often used in dishes like custard, cinnamon ice cream and dessert syrup. You will taste the difference in this amazing dessert.

Makes 4 churros

Ingredients
   1 recipe sweet dough
   1/2 teaspoon Ceylon cinnamon (found in Mexican markets, or use 1 teaspoon regular ground cinnamon)
   3 tablespoon granulated sugar
   2 teaspoons orange zest
   2 tablespoons butter, melted
   1/2 gallon vanilla ice cream
   Chocolate syrup for drizzling on top

Directions
   In a flat dish, combine cinnamon, sugar, and orange zest. Brush both side of the grilled piadina with melted butter, and roll both sides in the cinnamon mixture. Place churros on a plate with a scoop of ice cream in the center, and roll up and around the ice cream, pressing down to seal. Drizzle with chocolate syrup and serve.

INDEX

THE SKINNY BREAD COOKBOOK

C